Paul Harcourt is National Leader for New Wine, as well as leading All Saints' Woodford Wells in north-east London with his wife Becky. He is the author of two books on living the Spirit-filled life: *Growing in Circles* (River Publishing/New Wine, 2016) and, with Becky, *Walking on Water* (River Publishing/New Wine, 2017). Paul and Becky are involved in leadership training for renewed churches and regularly speak at conferences in the UK and Europe.

Ralph Turner is an author and biographer. Based in Leicester, he and his wife Rohini are part of Chroma Church. Ralph is Team Pastor for the evangelistic association Mission24 and he also serves as Chair of The Leprosy Mission, England and Wales.

EDITED BY
**PAUL HARCOURT
& RALPH TURNER**

GREATER THINGS

THE STORY OF NEW WINE SO FAR

Dedicated to David and Mary Pytches, whose faithfulness
and courage have inspired a generation

First published in Great Britain in 2019

Society for Promoting Christian Knowledge
36 Causton Street
London SW1P 4ST
www.spck.org.uk

British Library Cataloguing-in-Publication Data
A catalogue record for this book is available from the British Library

ISBN 978–0–281–08155–4
eBook ISBN 978–0–281–08156–1

1 3 5 7 9 10 8 6 4 2

Typeset by Fakenham Prepress Solutions, Fakenham, Norfolk NR21 8NL
First printed in Great Britain by Jellyfish Print Solutions

Subsequently digitally reprinted in Great Britain

eBook by Fakenham Prepress Solutions, Fakenham, Norfolk NR21 8NL

Produced on paper from sustainable forests

Contents

Foreword

For 13 consecutive years, Caroline and I spent a week of each summer at New Wine. Sometimes it was in a tent in the rain, sometimes in a caravan in the rain. It was always in the rain. I think Shepton Mallet, where we went, has a microclimate that ensures it always rains during New Wine.

Joking apart, during those 13 years, we were in a series of churches where the kind of worship, fellowship, prayer ministry and, above all, expectation was something to be learned rather than something we found. For those coming from ministry in a small church, New Wine was sometimes infuriating, a source of temptation to envy, but primarily a time where, by the end of the week, one was conscious of having met with Jesus and found fresh hope and calling.

If for nothing else – and there is an enormous amount else – New Wine would have justified its existence by this ministry to local churches, in terms of encouragement, hope and expectancy.

I want to pick up especially on that word 'expectancy'. There's a wonderful book that was written by Voltaire called *Candide*. Candide is about as naïve as they come. Voltaire's inspiration for most of the book came from Dr Pangloss, who proclaimed 'all is for the best in the best of all possible worlds'. The book is a comic but tragic account of Candide's travels through Europe, with Dr Pangloss and others, and almost everything that could go wrong does. At the end, the group of travellers settles down and says that all one can do is cultivate one's garden, look after one's own life.

That approach – of 'all is for the best in the best of all possible worlds' – is a caricature often seen as applying to New Wine.

The inspiration for New Wine sprang from the extra-ordinary ministry of John Wimber and his friendship with Bishop David Pytches, whose influence on the Church of England has not really been properly recognized. New Wine has developed and deepened and found its own life and path under successive leaders.

John Wimber's characteristics were absolute transparency, deep trust in Jesus (who found John when he was an adult) and a great belief in the promises of the New Testament.

New Wine has known its share of difficulties and failures – struggles to understand why people were not healed, the weaknesses of individuals and our common tendency to sin, pride and self-sufficiency. But that is not the point of this book, nor should it be. Its point is to celebrate the good things of Jesus Christ and, above all, his promise that we will see greater things. Its aim is to contribute to New Wine's decades-long mission of encouragement and the creation of expectancy that God is on the move, the Holy Spirit is present, life is given and we are moving towards the culmination of all things, in God's good time.

Many years ago, I was in my parish church on a course for training incumbents (those who have responsibility for training curates). At the same time, there was a week-long mission by

J John at Coventry Cathedral. We were all encouraged to go to it, much to my relief as large numbers of those in my own church were doing so. Towards the end, there was a discussion among those of us on the course. There was the normal amount of complaining. Then, at the end, a remarkable clergyman – not at all from a New Wine tradition – said, 'I agree with all the criticisms, but I tell you this, if I could get people coming up to receive communion with the same sense of expectancy that God would meet with them as I saw in Coventry Cathedral this week, I think I would feel that I had done a good job.'

This book will encourage expectancy that God is active, we can trust his word and he is faithful. The world is not all for the best, but it is, ultimately, all for Christ.

Justin Welby,
The Archbishop of Canterbury

Thank yous

Thank you to all who have contributed to this book, especially:

David and Mary Pytches   Bruce Collins
Barry and Mary Kissell   Captain Alan Price
John and Anne Coles   Heather Holgate
Margaret Maynard-Madley   Mark Melluish
Mike Pilavachi   James Roberts
Matt Redman   Naomi Graham
Tim Hughes   Debby Wright

Thanks also for the help given by:

Tanya Raybould
Jean Deudney

and the wonderful words of:

Linda Maslen
Chris Sayburn

Introduction

This is a story of faith. A story of grace, service and sacrifice. This is a story, ultimately, about God.

In the history of all God has done through New Wine there have been countless remarkable people. Some of their names will be well known to many; others have played crucial roles but not necessarily been seen or acknowledged in the same way. All would say that, notwithstanding the many leaps of faith and hours of sacrifice, what has happened has gone beyond any of their wildest dreams. Simply put, for some reason, God has been pleased to add his blessing. New Wine has been part of a greater renewal, just one of many streams, but one with a wonderful story to tell of how God is doing great things today.

Jesus often likened the kingdom of God to things that are small and insignificant at first but contain great potential. The kingdom of God is described as like a mustard seed, which can grow to become a great tree, larger than all the garden plants. It is like yeast, of which only a small amount is needed, but when worked, it spreads throughout the batch of dough and transforms its properties. It is like a small pearl, easily overlooked but of great price and worth making sacrifices to obtain. It is like the tiny flame of a candle, fragile but capable of driving back the darkness and providing lighting for everyone in an entire house. In many ways, the story of what God has done through New Wine is not about big personalities, dramatic events or grand strategies. Instead it is about a grass-roots transformation that is influencing the Church in the UK and, increasingly, around the world.

No book of this nature can present a definitive account of New Wine's history, far less the impact of what God has put into motion. I'm conscious that many people deserve far more credit than space has allowed, and many more deserve a mention and haven't received one. We have thousands of testimonies of lives transformed through receiving healing or experiencing signs and wonders, but only a few pages to share them in. The narrow scope of the book also means that it has not been possible to tell many of the stories of how people, having encountered God's love and power through New Wine, have been inspired to give their lives to mission, start charities, engage in campaigns, protect the environment or commit to any number of other kingdom causes. Whereas there was a time, not so long ago, when many churches were suspicious of any emphasis on social action or social justice, today, through a combination of kingdom theology and encountering God's love in the power of the Spirit, few churches would think of outreach and evangelism in terms that did not include practical action.

After 30 years of summer conferences, New Wine remains vibrant and growing. What God began has spread, there is an increasing emphasis on church planting, new areas of ministry are emerging . . . but the essential DNA remains the same: encountering the presence of God in worship, a desire for the spiritual gifts with which Jesus equips his Church for mission, prayer ministry in the power of the Holy Spirit, and an overflow of love to our communities through local churches.

It always has been – and always will be – all about God, but we all have our part to play. Jesus said that whoever believed in him would do the things that he was doing, indeed even greater things (John 14.12). The kingdom that Jesus inaugurated is continuing to grow, and I trust that this book will inspire and encourage you to join in.

Paul Harcourt

Jesus said: 'Believe me when I say that I am in the Father and the Father is in me; or at least believe on the evidence of the works themselves. Very truly I tell you, whoever believes in me will do the works I have been doing, and they will do even *greater things* than these, because I am going to the Father' (John 14.11-12, italics added).

1   Beginnings

Bishop David Pytches and his wife Mary were the pioneers of New Wine. Here David tells how it all began.

New Wine's story has been a great adventure. In so far as I have a part to play, I want to say at the very beginning that I love the story and the testimonies but will take no credit for the movement at all. All I did was to share a vision that God gave me – to impart what I felt the Lord had shown me. Others have done the work.

It seems to me that God always had his hand on my life – and I am so grateful for that. My father was a rector in the Church of England and a number of my relatives were members of the clergy. Even the fact that my name is David impressed on me from an early age that God had called me to lead. My father used to say that our primary call is to seek the will of God, and then to stay in the centre of that will. As I sought God, I knew from my early schooldays that I was called to serve God in the Church.

I went to a college in Bristol, established by the Bible Churchmen's Missionary Society. It trained missionaries and, although I had no desire to be one, there is no doubt that the move was of God's making. While at college, I met a lot of ex-servicemen who had really proved the Lord's goodness during the Second

World War. Meeting these men had a great impact on me. It made me realize that I had led a very sheltered life as a Christian and I needed to spend my National Service in the ranks to see something of the other side of life. I joined the army and became a sergeant instructor in the Royal Army Educational Corps.

MARY

Following my time in the army, and after a final year at college, I joined St Ebbe's Church in Oxford. Being responsible for the youth work, I couldn't help noticing a girl called Mary Trevisick. She was a natural at welcoming people. I was fascinated by her outgoing nature.

I remember needing to buy some pots and pans for my house at the time. I decided to take Mary with me as I hoped she might know more than I did about what to get. I asked the salesperson for help and she responded with an interesting question.

'Well, can I ask how many children there are?'

I was fond of Mary. And I was a bit mischievous too. I turned to her and said: 'Mary, how many children would you like?'

It was the oddest of proposals, I suppose. Mary went away to ponder my words. We married in 1958.

Before we married, we talked together about the mission field. I told her that I had no desire to go, but I must be willing to do so if God called me. To be honest, I hoped he wouldn't call me! Mary said she felt exactly the same.

By 1959, with our first daughter Charlotte in our arms, we were on a ship, sailing to Chile. Our destination was Cholchol in the province of Cautin. The South American Missionary Society had a mission, school and hospital there. One of our first jobs was to gather the Christians together for a conference – our first toe in the water of organization and an early picture of what God would do through us with the formation of New Wine.

CHURCH PLANTING

Those early days in Chile were not very easy. We were dealing with an entirely different world. The culture shock was enormous. Everything from having to face fleas, rats and earthquakes through to drawing water from a well and there being only three hours of electricity a day.

After two and a half years, we were called to pioneer church planting in the port of Valparaiso, where we had first disembarked, and then extend the work to the regions around. Church planting! We really had no idea as to what was entailed, let alone how to do it.

We made our home in the local Anglican church building, converting part of it into bedrooms and a living room. We started with a local radio broadcast, which brought listeners to the church services. But with no one to teach us how to plant churches, and with no money, no Bibles and no buildings, it was a tough assignment.

We heard of a new housing estate. It was being built in a place called Gomez Carreno and I went up there with a Chilean pastor to walk around the whole site and claim it for the Lord. We had no idea at the time as to how God would fulfil those prayers. A year or so later, a lady from our church who was now living in one of those new houses asked me to go up and bless her home. Having prayed around the house, we relaxed with a cup of tea. It was then that the lady suggested something outrageous.

'Pastor, we really should have a church on this estate. There are forty thousand new residents coming into this area!'

'Yes, I can see that, but where would we hold the meetings? We have no money for a building.'

'Here. Here, Pastor! In this room!'

The thought had never occurred to me. Church in the home. What a novel concept! Again, without knowing it, God was preparing me for all he wanted to do once we got back to the UK.

The church blossomed. Many people came to Christ, and eventually they outgrew the largest of the living rooms and built their own new building.

THE HOLY SPIRIT

As much as we were learning from the Lord about church planting and house church, he had us on another journey as well. After a break in the UK, we returned by ship to Argentina, then

David and Mary Pytches with children, San Pablo, Chile, 1967

travelled on to Chile. But on that journey, Mary was desperate for change in her own walk with God.

While on the ship, she prayed to God: 'O God, I can't get off this boat the way I'm getting on.'

Mary had been reading the Rees Howells biography *Intercessor*,[1] and it had a significant effect on her. In addition, we had both been exposed to the ministries of the Pentecostal churches in South America and, if we were honest, we knew something was missing in our own lives.

One night, lying in our bunks on the ship, Mary made an announcement.

'David, God has done an amazing thing. He has baptized me in the Holy Spirit!'

Once again, I was taken by surprise. My reply at the time was along the lines of being pleased for her. But what Mary had experienced was life-changing and I wanted it too.

Back in Chile, I spoke with her.

'Darling, it's made such an incredible difference to you and to our marriage; I just need you to pray for me too.'

Mary prayed. And God the Holy Spirit did his work.

At the time the Lord was filling us and blessing us with his Holy Spirit, I was experiencing one of my more difficult moments in ministry. My bishop was a good man, but unable and seemingly unwilling to help with church planting. I was ready for a meeting and had a long list as to what was wrong with him! However, with the baptism of the Holy Spirit came more of an awareness of the gentle voice of the Spirit. I was reminded of the passage in 1 Corinthians 13: '[love] keeps no record of wrongs'. Our meeting became a time of marvellous reconciliation and directly led to a mini-revival in some of the churches.

Other church leaders approached me and asked why it was that some churches were being blessed with growth, both in numbers and in relation to their walk with God. My answer became the watchword of my life: 'Catch the fire!'

By God's grace, the fire caught! Churches up and down Chile were on fire for God. One Saturday stays in my mind. We baptized around a hundred people in a local river. This was baptism by full immersion – a far cry from the christenings we were used to in the Anglican Church back in the UK.

Along the way, I became Bishop for the whole diocese of Chile, Bolivia and Peru. Despite political revolutions in some of the countries I represented, God's revolution was greater. Lives were changed. People were added to the Church. Many were baptized in the Holy Spirit. There was no doubt about it. We were catching the fire.

2 A moment in time

As David and Mary Pytches returned to the UK, they knew they wanted to take further steps to honour God by sharing what they had learned of the ministry of the Holy Spirit. The catalyst for this was the visit of John Wimber. Ralph Turner explains.

In 1977, having returned from Chile, David and Mary Pytches began working with St Andrew's Church, Chorleywood. They were encouraged that they had found a church which was already beginning to respond to the working of the Holy Spirit, particularly through the ministry of Barry and Mary Kissell. David describes how he 'inherited' Barry as a member of staff[1] and as someone already active in the work and power of the Holy Spirit. As Director of Faith Sharing, Barry would regularly take out teams in order to minister and encourage, and over the years this had resulted in reaching hundreds of other churches and many nations.[2]

Arriving at Chorleywood, David and Mary were excited but unsure about how to take things forward. As David put it, 'in my ignorance of how to coordinate renewal I soon began to feel that something good was slipping out of our grasp.'[3]

Within a short period of time David heard the name 'John Wimber' from two different sources. One comment was from the church growth expert Eddie Gibbs (originally a member of St Andrew's). The other was from David's friend from St Michael le Belfrey in York, David Watson. A remark from David Watson was particularly telling for David Pytches: David Watson felt that his encounter with John Wimber meant that his ministry would never be the same again.[4] David and Mary wanted to find out more.

It turned out that David Watson had invited John Wimber to speak at York, so David Pytches contacted John to invite him to stop over at St Andrew's Chorleywood on the way. David cheekily suggested that Chorleywood was 'conveniently near Heathrow'![5] The invitation was accepted.

HEATHROW

John was hard to miss at Heathrow. Although later in life he slimmed down, he was, by his own self-deprecating admission, a 'fat man going to heaven'.[6] John Gunstone describes him in a meeting as follows: 'He wore jeans, a big belt round an ample stomach and an open-necked lumberjack's shirt. His large round face was haloed by greying hair – a Britisher's image of a trapper from the Rockies.'[7]

Image aside, David Pytches had a more pressing problem as he drove John from Heathrow. It turned out that John had brought with him 29 other people, who were staying in London and would travel up for the meetings.

'I think there's been a misunderstanding, John.'

'Why? What's the matter?'

'Well, I invited you to come. I didn't realize there would be a team as well.'

'Does that matter, David?'

'Well, no, except I just don't know how we're going to pay you. I had budgeted for you, but thirty air fares from California . . .'

'Oh no, David! Don't worry about that. We feel the Lord called us to come. All I would say is this: if God blesses you, give it away.'[8]

David was relieved of course. He had expected that St Andrew's would cover the expenses, along with David Watson's church, but never anticipated such a large team! He learned something about generosity that day that has stayed with him.

The meetings at St Andrew's were life-changing.

GOD WANTS HIS CHURCH BACK

David Pytches remembers those first John Wimber meetings in June 1981[9] as if it was yesterday. John's laid-back style was accompanied by a powerful presence of the Holy Spirit. As John spoke, David was transfixed by the message. For too long, John said, we have been running church our way. But God wants his Church back.[10]

One of John's team spoke at the first meeting. Mark Melluish was there. Now a church leader and one of New Wine's leaders for many years, at that time Mark was an accredited member of the 'back-row boys'. It's fair to say he did not have the strongest of Christian faiths at the time: 'There was a group of us who sat on the back row so we could chat and watch others, and any time it came to the talk, we would enjoy passing notes to one another or making comment.'[11]

That evening Mark began to change. He recalls John Wimber speaking with strong faith and authority. Wimber was certain that God could heal and that the healing could happen there and then. Mark could not remember hearing anyone speak with such certainty before. It got his attention.

John Wimber believed in Holy Spirit supernatural encounters. He saw them as 'divine appointments', demonstrated through the likes of signs, wonders, healing and deliverance.[12] In the meeting, he began to bring words of knowledge, and numbers of people were responding. But for Mark, it wasn't enough – none of the responses could really be proven. For example, someone claimed to have been released from significant back pain, but there could be no visible proof of that. But this was about to change:

> The meeting had gone on for a long time. We'd started at 6.30 and were now heading towards 9 o'clock. At that point, one of the men in church pushed his wife forwards in a wheelchair – she was unable to walk. Another woman stepped forward who was blind. I'd done some work for the woman who had no sight, in her garden, so I knew that she really was blind and that she couldn't see anything. And my sceptical mind thought, 'Well, let's see what happens now.'
>
> John Wimber didn't seem too fazed. He started to pray for both of these women. As he prayed for the one who was blind, she began to describe her eyesight coming back. She described blurred figures and at that we were all caught up, listening in to John's prayerful conversation with her as he encouraged her again and again to step forward in faith and to trust that God would be at work that day.

Suddenly the lady who was blind was quiet. Everyone waited.

'I can see you! I can see![13] I see a fat man!'

Everyone burst into laughter – John Wimber was indeed somewhat overweight.

John then began to pray for the woman in the wheelchair. In Mark's words:

John asked us to join in – she had multiple sclerosis [MS] and we knew her well. Her husband, an amazing man, had been faithfully pushing her around and looking after her. Their relationship was beautiful. It was beautiful to see a marriage that was obviously made in heaven, a marriage that had gone through difficult times. It was a marriage where it was 'for better or worse', and this illness was obviously difficult for them both.

John encouraged the lady to trust and to believe that God could do something – to trust and make herself vulnerable to the presence of the Holy Spirit in this new and exciting way that God had promised at the beginning of the service. Mark stared open-mouthed as the woman began to stand. Mark recalls: 'The lady got up out of her wheelchair and began to walk. We laughed and cheered as she pushed her husband, who had climbed into the wheelchair, out of the church.'

Over the weekend, there were other significant healings. David Pytches recalls a lady paralysed in both hands being completely healed. As a result, she was able to return to work as a secretary and to begin to teach again at the children's Sunday school.[14]

DO THE SAME

As the weekend progressed, David had time to reflect on the meetings and on John Wimber's style of teaching. David saw the Spirit of God come upon many of the young people. As David expresses it:

Because he gave time and silent space for the Holy Spirit to do something (which was a totally novel thing to me) I could

> see he was in no way whipping up emotions and it certainly
> didn't violate any of my biblical perceptions. I felt happy to
> let God be God.[15]

Many lives were radically changed over that weekend. People
fell to the floor as the Spirit touched them, with one member of
the American team pointing to the part of the room that was to
receive the power of the Spirit next.[16] One young man outside
the church building was unable to enter because of the force
meeting him from inside as he approached the doors.[17] For some
at the meetings, it is a time remembered for a healing received.
For others, it was faith restored. As for Mark Melluish, he would
never be the same again:

> No longer was I this sceptical, hesitant believer listening to
> well-meaning words that said 'God is there for you'. Now
> we had an understanding that God was there and would act
> and was on your side. And you could ask for anything and
> he could do something new in our lives.
>
> It was an evening that changed my life and began to
> change the course of the Church in this country.

John Wimber emphasized that the kingdom of God really was
'good news'. To demonstrate this, in most of the meetings, he
moved into times of prayer and healing. The members of his
team from the USA would then begin to move around the church
building, praying for people. By the end of that weekend, there
had been many baptized in the Spirit and a good number of
healings. But what stays with David Pytches is the memory of
what happened to his own church members.

The American visitors were not just ministering but also
demonstrating. They were showing believers how to pray and

inviting them to do the same. Those meetings brought 'a much broader expression and experience of the work of the Spirit'.[18]

James Roberts, now leading a church plant called Connect Church Chorleywood, was at that first meeting too. He recalls the teaching as 'unremarkable'. But it's what happened next that James most remembers. The team with John Wimber began to pray for those in the congregation to be empowered to pray and to heal in the same way:

> [The American team members] joined hands with some of my friends from the youth group and they started crying, convulsing and shaking as if electricity was flowing through them. I could hear their teeth chattering from where I was sitting (hiding) a few rows back from the front. Another friend was jumping up and down like he was riding a pogo stick in the corner. Other members of the team were praying for the sick and a lady in a wheelchair.
>
> It seemed like complete chaos had been unleashed on our nice normal church and to be honest I was more than a little unnerved by it all.
>
> My friends talked of being overcome by waves of love, and feeling power course through their bodies. That evening shattered my theology and opened up a whole new spiritual realm right before my eyes.[19]

One of those young people was Andrew Burkes. Andrew noticed that Claire, his girlfriend, began to shake and that others were responding in the same way. As Andrew took Claire's hand, he felt what he could only describe as a 'love and power' flow over him. He saw a vision of Jesus in front of him, and began to weep. For Andrew, it was a transforming moment as he asked God to change his life once and for all.[20]

THE ANOINTED TEAM

As a result of those meetings, and the prayer for members of their congregation, David and Mary Pytches had 18 of their own congregation anointed in a new way with a Holy Spirit gift of healing.

Mary recalls:

> That weekend turned our church upside-down. It turned us upside-down. I don't think either of us would ever be the same again. We were so excited by the end of that weekend. We'd seen a whole new dimension of ministry. We'd seen the possibility of power evangelism, we'd seen people being healed, we watched blind eyes being opened, we'd just seen incredible things. We'd seen a whole bunch of young people being filled with the Spirit in the most amazing way. We were really excited and the church just took off after that.[21]

Barry Kissell, one of the leaders, was away for most of the weekend. He remembers what happened when his wife, Mary, returned from the Wimber meetings:

> When I returned home, it was late and yet my wife, Mary, was still at the church. When she came in she looked quite different and asked me if I minded if she just sat quietly by herself on the sofa. She sat with her eyes closed and her hands before her in an open position. I sat with her into the early hours. I have never felt such peace and power emanating from a person before, not to mention the heat! . . . The next morning, Mary told me that John Wimber had welcomed the Holy Spirit, that God was anointing people for a healing ministry and that the sign was their hot and tingling hands. It was at that moment [in the meeting] that

Mary felt something like a powerful electric current running through her hands. She went to the front with the rest and was anointed with oil, whereupon the fire of God swept through her whole body; this was the anointing that burned in her all night.[22]

John Wimber records that the Sunday evening meeting was the most powerful meeting he had experienced outside his own church.[23]

After the weekend, David Pytches rang his daughter Debby, who was away at university, and told her what had happened.

He told her how a lady with MS who had been in a wheelchair for years, well known to the congregation, had got up out of her chair and walked round the church. Blind eyes had been opened. He told her about how the unchurched young people who hung around the car park came in to see what the commotion was about and met God. As a result, a number gave their lives to Jesus (including one who then went on to marry Debby's sister).

Debby had become anorexic and bulimic and far from church. As she heard David telling her this over the phone, she prayed, 'Lord, I just want to come home.' She felt touched by the Holy Spirit in that moment and went from the phone box straight back to her university friends, who were far from the Lord, and told them that Jesus heals. One of her friends was at that point very ill in the university sick bay, so Debby's friends challenged her to go and pray. She did and the sick friend was instantly healed!

This experience had such an impact on Debby and her boyfriend John (Wright) that they stopped living together, got engaged and 'vowed' to make it to the next John Wimber visit.

When they arrived, John Wimber was playing the piano. There was something so tangible about God's presence that Debby just started crying as the Lord did a deep work emotionally. John found himself shaking, which he had never done before, and deeply affected by the Holy Spirit. Later in the meeting, Debby went forward when a word of knowledge was given about someone with a torn ligament in the thigh. As she was prayed for, she fell down under the Spirit for a long time and the ligament was completely healed.

News travelled. Soon, busloads of people were turning up at St Andrew's Chorleywood, seeking more of the Holy Spirit. The original ministry team of 18 people who had been commissioned after Wimber's visit were clearly not sufficient and, within a few months, as many as 250 people were ministering in different ways, in what John Wimber had called 'body ministry'.[24] As Wimber has quipped: 'everybody gets to play!'[25]

One of those who experienced the impact of the early visits of John Wimber was a young evangelist called J John:

> John Wimber brought a freshness, a simplicity and a heart-warming worship and ministry. It felt like having a good drink of water, not realizing how thirsty we were. I felt renewed and refreshed. John and I became good friends and I spoke at several of his pastors' conferences at his church in Anaheim, California, and led two evangelistic missions there. He was passionate about Christ and about making Christ known.[26]

David Pytches' own thinking and approach to ministry was reshaped by John Wimber's visit.[27] He would not be the same because of it. Nor could the church be the same. Healing was for the Church today. It didn't have to be just for ministers operating in their ministry. Every believer could pray for the sick. Every believer could testify to Christ's salvation. This was God the Holy Spirit moving powerfully. And David was clear: this had to go beyond the walls of St Andrew's.

3 Renewal

As the impact of John Wimber's ministry began to be shared by David Pytches and St Andrew's, many other church leaders experienced the same transformation. John Coles recalls those early days of the renewal movement. John led New Wine from 2001 to 2014 and continues as Chair of Trustees for New Wine.

My new journey in the Spirit had begun when I realized how little I was achieving in leading the Church of St Barnabas, Woodside Park, London. I had previously served two curacies at large and growing Evangelical churches and thought that I knew how to lead a growing church. How wrong I was. After a year of frustration that my 'sound preaching' and best attempts at good pastoral leadership were bearing no fruit, I came to the end of my own resources and began crying out to God that 'there must be more than this'! After six months of frustrated prayer, I asked our friends John and Eleanor Mumford to pray for me to be filled afresh with the Spirit, and God graciously overwhelmed me with his loving presence and power.

I was hungry for God and I genuinely wanted to lead people to faith and see the Church grow. Probably there was also an underlying sense of not wanting to be seen to be a 'failing leader'.

As they prayed, I found myself being overwhelmed by God's presence and love, and literally physically shaken by his power. As they prophesied over me, I began to realize that God was so much more compassionate and merciful than I had previously thought and Jesus was much more able to lead his Church than I was!

I was introduced to John Wimber's teaching tapes about the kingdom, the Spirit and church planting. The teaching was so refreshing and was genuinely challenging the way we did things. I wanted to hear more. I had not been around for his first visit to Chorleywood and York, but in 1984, I went to California to his conference at Anaheim, 'Signs and Wonders and Church Growth', and then immediately booked a place at the first big public conference he led in England at Westminster Central Hall. These John Wimber meetings had been arranged at the invitation of David Pytches. It was after these meetings that my wife Anne and I met with David and Mary. They became informal mentors and spiritual parents to us as we soaked up a whole new approach to Christian ministry.

THE MENTOR GROUP

Soon after that, our friends John Mumford, who was at that stage a curate in the Anglican Church, and his wife Eleanor convened a small group of church leaders and their spouses. They invited David and Mary Pytches to mentor the group, which met about every six weeks for a period of 18 months. My wife Anne and I were privileged to be invited to this somewhat select and eclectic group. At these meetings, Anne found herself being asked to lead worship on her guitar, and David would then speak from Scripture and invite the Spirit to come in power to minister to us. Invariably we encountered God in a life-transforming and healing way. David's ministry had been remodelled following the early visit from John Wimber and, with John's encouragement, he was beginning to document what the Holy Spirit was doing; this found its way into print eventually as *Come Holy Spirit*.[1]

The ministry from John Wimber and his team, coupled with the ongoing meetings and mentoring with David and Mary Pytches, resulted in our need to begin to change the way we worked and the way we led our church. Most of us in the mentor group were experiencing significant opposition to this new theological emphasis on the Holy Spirit and to the practices we were introducing into our churches. We needed to learn how to forgive those who were opposing, criticizing and hurting us.

Anne recalls crying copious tears during a ministry time at one of our meetings:

> I was unable to express verbally the pain and frustration of receiving accusatory and hostile words from members of the congregation who did not understand nor want to follow John's leadership of the church as he learned about the Holy Spirit. Even those we thought might support us, because they had had similar spiritual experiences, doubted our wisdom and integrity. It seemed as if we were at an impasse and I was in despair, hoping for some comfort or reassurance. Into this soggy mess stepped David Pytches who simply whispered in my ear, 'You must forgive them!' It was both a word of knowledge, since he didn't know why I was crying, and a word of wisdom, since that was the only way out of my predicament. Hard as it was, I spoke out before the Lord my forgiveness to the faces in my memory, and the Lord brought instant comfort and release.

We needed a safe place to express our frustrations and feelings. Like Anne, I would often end up weeping on the carpet at some stage in the mentor meetings. Then we would leave and go back to the fray, strengthened in the Lord.

LEADERSHIP MODEL

These meetings were, in a sense, the prototype of future New Wine Network meetings, giving us a model for leaders' meetings that were neither competitive nor cynical. In my own experience, meetings with other Evangelicals were often characterized by competition, where biblical orthodoxy and church size were the highly sought after and prized commodities. In contrast, our local clergy meetings were often characterized by cynicism; those who had probably entered the ministry with great faith, hopes and dreams were now resigned to declining church attendance and influence. The weekly attritional demands of leading a church into a ministry and mission appropriate for the post-Christian culture of twentieth-century Britain were proving too much. Sadly for them, it appeared easier to become a sort of spiritual social worker, cynical about the possibility of conversion to Christ and about transformation through the power of the Holy Spirit.

Since all forms of natural life thrive in the right environment, it's important to ask the question, 'What is the right environment in which church leaders can grow in faith, skill, wisdom and courage?' I concluded that, for me, and for many others, it would be through meeting frequently with others who have a similar vision and values. That's why those early meetings convened by John and Eleanor Mumford were so precious.

Coming into this new experience of the Holy Spirit, I realized very quickly that my ecclesiology, not just my theology, would have to change. In other words, I couldn't just be a quiet Charismatic, creating a small group (or holy huddle) that would experience the Spirit in new ways but leave the rest of the church membership untouched. This renewal was intended for everyone and for every area of church life – God wanted to renew our worship, our prayer lives, our teaching and preaching, our training of lay people, our small groups, our leadership structures, our giving, our marriages, our raising of our children, our work in the community, our involvement in world mission . . . the list is almost endless. I realized that I wouldn't be able to bring about the changes that were necessary without the help of friends committed to the same renewed vision and on the same learning journey.

TRAINING DAYS

I found great support and friendship when I plugged into the training days for church leaders that David Pytches began to run at Chorleywood two or three times a year, starting in the mid-1980s. They were a natural extension of the earlier meetings and they became a place where I could hear others teach and encourage. We spoke on the principles of prophecy, healing, evangelism, communication and leadership, and were able to discuss the issues they raised as friends in a safe environment. This was also a place where I could worship with others without having the responsibility of leading or overseeing or of subsequently reviewing that worship; it was just a great place to encounter God afresh. It was a place where I could be prayed for in the power of the Spirit. On most occasions, God would reveal some area of hurt or need, either through the teaching or through a prophetic revelation when I went forward for prayer. Painful as it was at times, I was learning that most renewal in the Church has to begin with renewal in the pastor! And this was also a place I could take others from our church leadership team to learn a new way of being church.

Following on from the early John Wimber meetings, David held a residential conference for church leaders, together with Anglican Renewal Ministries (ARM), in Swanwick.[2] He invited Anne and me to go and tell the story of what God was doing at St Barnabas and we gladly went, mainly to learn more rather than thinking that we had very much to say. It became clear that ARM was potentially too Anglican for David and he realized he would need to start a new thing in order to propagate more quickly and more widely what God had put on his heart. He also realized that while some leaders were applying lessons very quickly in their own churches, they were often experiencing significant opposition from their church members. It was not enough to meet as leaders – we needed to convey to our congregations the wonder of what God was doing by his Holy Spirit. David's solution was to bring leaders and people together into a family conference. New Wine '89 was born.

SEED MONEY

David had been given some seed money by John Wimber for such an adventure of faith, and also wrote to ten other church leaders to ask if they would each invest £1,000. Sadly our church, though asked to contribute, was not in a position to do so since it was still too divided over this renewal. Instead, we took about 25 to 30 of our congregation, including children, to the first event. St Barnabas has been thoroughly involved in New Wine ever since.

This also accorded with a vision through which the Lord had spoken to me when he called me to be ordained. I was driving down the M1 with a clergy friend and we were talking about what I would do when I finished my engineering degree. I had discovered that my first love was not engineering but sharing my faith in Jesus, and I had already had a conversation with my friend about the possibility of ordination. Now I suddenly became aware of the towers and steeples of the village churches that I could see as we sped past them on the motorway. I began to think: what would happen if a biblically based vicar was in every pulpit and leading every church? The nation would be changed! From that moment I knew I had to offer myself as one of them . . . and the Church of England was subsequently foolish enough to accept me as an ordinand.

Once ordained, that vision was buried in my subconscious. But then, in 1991, an American Vineyard church pastor, Bob Craine, came to lead a conference in our church. He asked the Spirit to unearth buried and unfulfilled dreams – and God awoke the vision. As I stood at the front of the church and the Spirit came, suddenly the vision was recalled as freshly as it had first been received. Within weeks, Teddy Saunders (who had retired from being Vicar of St Michael's Chester Square, and was living in Chorleywood and helping David Pytches) invited me to help with retreats designed to introduce church leaders to the renewing power of the Spirit. From then on, I became more connected with the river of renewal flowing from Chorleywood around the country. When David Pytches subsequently invited me to lead the New Wine team, I felt it was in order to fulfil that dream of seeing renewal in every church and to see revival in the UK.

My personal experience of leading a middle-of-the-road sleepy liberal suburban Anglican church into Charismatic renewal enabled me to empathize with many other leaders who were facing difficulties as they tried to do the same thing. For some of the leaders on the retreats at Chorleywood, the model of church life that the Spirit had generated was already too developed for them to think, *I could do that* back home. So Teddy Saunders would bring the participants over for a morning to see another church with a much less experienced vicar than David Pytches who would then tell the story of leading change and renewal. Often people would reflect on their experience of Sunday worship at St Andrew's, commenting on how relatively 'normal' it was but wanting to know how to get from where they were to where they wanted to be. They could learn from some of the stepping stones I had discovered – as well as how to avoid falling off, as I had often done! Others on the course had expected something very intense and way beyond their ability to lead, but they were discovering our value of being *naturally supernatural and supernaturally natural*. David would sometimes say, 'There is nothing that puts people off more than over-intensity.' We wanted all the participants to have a new encounter with God, have a new theology of God at work and see a model of church life such that they could leave feeling, 'I could do this too.'

WINESKINS

Most of what I taught was on 'the pitfalls I fell into that you can avoid'. One of the simplest lessons, which I only learned through failure, was that Jesus said: 'No-one pours new wine into old wineskins. If he does, the wine will burst the skins, and both the wine and the wineskins will be ruined.'[3] I had tried to bring change into the main morning service because I so longed for the church to be accessible to other families like our own. But I experienced tremendous opposition to the modern music, the informality, biblical preaching, the focus on personal encounter with God and prayer ministry, and the inclusion of families with young people.

We now recommend that leaders should establish a new congregation alongside the old, to reach previously unreached people in the neighbourhood. Additionally, gaining permission from a reluctant parish church council or eldership for an 'experimental period' is often easier than an open-ended permission. Successful experiments can last a long time and, since God loves doing new things, and adds life to new life, we now have a lot of long-term experiments! Creating a new wineskin is much better for collecting new members (wine) and doesn't break the hearts or the preferred worship patterns (wineskins) of the previous generation.

In fact, what we were teaching was all about New Wine.

4 Gathering

Author and biographer Ralph Turner investigates the beginnings of New Wine as people met together at that very first gathering in August 1989.

It was a hot day. That first Monday, 7 August 1989, the start of the very first New Wine gathering, was cloudless. As people queued to register, an ice-cream van arrived. A speculative move on the part of the driver resulted in a roaring trade as the temperatures soared through that hot afternoon.[1]

Tents were going up in prearranged 'villages', each reflective of churches and parishes. A number of mission organizations were setting up their wares. Children raced up and down the field after a black-and-white spotted football. There were shrieks of laughter from the bouncy castle. And wherever you walked, there was a buzz of conversation.

The marquees were already in position, left over from a Bible Week from the week before whose organizers had agreed to cooperate with this new initiative.

As the sound of worship leader Andy Park's guitar reached the far corners of the Royal Bath and West Showground in the early evening, people began to gather. The hoped-for number of attendees was 1,500, which was the break-even figure. In fact 3,500 turned up. And New Wine was born.

But let's go back in time.

REACHING EVERYBODY

Two years earlier, David Pytches had been having a conversation with some of his fellow leaders.

'We have to reach everybody, not just the leaders!'

David's comments came from a sense of frustration with the reception some congregations were giving to the move of God that was resulting from the John Wimber meetings and subsequent gatherings.

David, working with Barry Kissell, had initiated a number of leaders' meetings. These had been dynamic times, with a clear Holy Spirit anointing. But leaders were finding it hard to translate this to their regular congregations on a Sunday. And on the occasions when members of congregations were visiting renewal meetings, they were then experiencing similar frustrations when their leaders didn't seem to share the same enthusiasm.

'What if we could get everyone together – leaders and congregations – all in one place?' David mused.

Some of the leaders had attended a Bible Week during that summer of 1987 and this was a further catalyst for ideas – perhaps they should start something similar.

There seemed, to the leaders, to be something of a 'God-direction' on this. Plans began. Conversations took place: what if we started a summer camp? What if we gave ourselves a couple of years and planned for the summer of 1989? What if we found a showground or a racecourse that could accommodate us? What if we sent out leaflets to all our contacts?

Would people come? Was it possible? Where would the money come from?

Those first meetings had far more questions than answers.

FIND A PLACE, FIND A NAME

'Let's keep praying about this,' said David. 'And let's push some doors. We need to find a place and find a name!'

Margaret Maynard-Madley, David's secretary, and Mike Pilavachi, youth leader at St Andrew's, were sent out to find an appropriate venue. A look at Cheltenham Racecourse proved unpromising, but someone mentioned the possibility of the Royal Bath and West Showground at Shepton Mallet in Somerset.

Meeting the showground coordinator resulted in a far more fruitful conversation. It turned out that there was already a Bible Week on the site in late July. The coordinator suggested that there might be some synergy between the two weeks, with the loan of marquees and equipment.

Phone calls followed, and within a short time an agreement had been reached for the organizers of the Bible Week to loan their equipment, with marquees already in place for the first of the new gatherings.

But a name was still needed. David Pytches had suggested 'Anglicans Awake'. This hadn't gone down so well. Mike Pilavachi recalls that it was on a Sunday afternoon walk with Bob Maynard and Margaret Maynard-Madley that the name was first mentioned:

> I remember one day David Pytches asked Margaret to start to administrate the week and we went for a walk one Sunday after lunch. We were trying to think of a name – I remember all sorts of ridiculous-sounding names! In the end it was Bob Maynard who said that as it's gonna be '89, why don't we call

> it New Wine '89? I think I remember saying, 'Yeah, that's
> great, but we'll have to think of another name for '90.' I was
> wrong on that one![2]

The name stuck because of the wider connotations with new
wine and new wineskins.[3] Mike recalls:

> The honest truth was it was New Wine that rhymed with
> '89. I mean, at least in part, and of course it was because it
> meant something as well: new wine, new wineskins. The
> honest truth was we were walking in a field and it was
> suddenly, 'Well, that's that then.' That's it.

NO MONEY

The next problem was finance. David Pytches had been given
some seed money by John Wimber for such an adventure of faith,
and David also wrote to ten other church leaders to ask if they
would each invest £1,000. Not all did, but there was enough of
a response for the venture to move forward.

In June 1988 it was formally announced that New Wine '89
would be taking place the following summer.[4]

The first office was in Bob Maynard and Margaret Maynard-
Madley's dining room. Margaret recalls:

> We had a telephone number fitted just for the conference.
> We had one computer which in those days was not fully used
> as a computer but more like an electric typewriter! Boxes
> of brochures and envelopes began to take over the room.
> Through the faith-sharing ministry led by Barry Kissell we
> had a few hundred names and addresses of leaders to whom
> we could send brochures. Also John Wimber gave David his
> mailing list used for conferences to contact. So there were
> several thousand to send out. I needed help to stuff envelopes

and several friends from church were co-opted. Adverts went into the Christian press – and so the word was out.

I realized we would need a lot of workers to make this happen! I went up for prayer at the end of one of the services, asking the Lord to supply the help, wisdom, imagination and all I needed for this task which was beginning to overwhelm me. Jeannie Morgan prayed for me and afterwards she asked me if I would like her to come to help in the office. This was the beginning of a partnership in organizing the whole event.

PLANNING THE EVENT

Planning now got under way in earnest. David and Mary Pytches, along with Barry and Mary Kissell, were to co-host the event. The site crew would mainly be from St Andrew's. Andy Park from Vineyard Canada, along with his band, were to lead the worship. Captain Alan Price from the Church Army was in place to run the children's events, and Mike Pilavachi, still feeling fairly 'green' and untested, agreed to take on the youth work. Outside speakers would include John Hughes, formerly a curate at St Andrew's, and Bob Hopkins, a faith-sharing colleague of Barry.[5]

A unique feature of the event was the large ministry team. This separated it from other Bible Weeks and Christian events. It offered those attending a special place to find a deeper walk with God. It offered prayer, ministry and inner healing in a way that was unlikely to be possible in the local church. The ministry emphasis had come from observations of meetings at St Andrew's. Mary Pytches explains:

> We had about 250 [trained in counselling and healing following the John Wimber meetings] in the end because

we had so much ministry going on. Conferences, day conferences, leadership conferences . . . we started retreats for clergy and we'd been ministering to them, so we needed a big ministry team. But what I began to discover was that, though we were in a sort of middle class area and no longer working amongst the poor [as we were in Chile], it doesn't mean to say people don't have any problems. In fact they were much deeper problems. So people would turn up on my doorstep for a cup of coffee and a good cry and I'd pray for them. But I began to think, I need to know how to help them more than I'm doing. This isn't enough. So I started to do some counselling courses with CWR, Selwyn Hughes' organisation; anything that was going actually.

We started what we called first of all, Prayer Counselling but later we called it Pastoral Prayer Ministry. That 250 ministry team who prayed with people on a Sunday and at conferences was also the team for when the New Wine conferences started; they were the team we took down to New Wine. They were the early team there. We drew out of that people with maturity and good biblical grounding who really had a heart for people's problems and we started training people to be able to pray with people on a longer term basis and during the week. We had about 25-30 couples that did that.[6]

That first week also saw a ministry towards married couples. Barry and Mary Kissell led the seminars together. Mary Kissell recalls:

The marriage seminar was the highlight of the early New Wines. At the end of the sessions, those who were unable to conceive were prayed for, and at the start of the next year those who had been blessed with babies as a result presented them. It gave hope to others.[7]

Alongside ministry, there was to be a strong emphasis on renewal in the meetings, of course. And there were discussions with and influence from a number of other streams, including Roger Forster and Ichthus Fellowship in the UK, and Vineyard from the USA and Canada.

THE START

Early on the first day, David Pytches led a prayer walk around the site, claiming it for the Lord, praying that everything that would happen in the week to come would glorify God. There was a strong sense of expectation among the crew serving on site.

'Excitement' and 'anticipation' were the words that came to mind as people arrived and registered for the event. The sun in the sky helped that first day to be one of celebration on many levels.

As the ice-cream man drove off site and Andy Park began to lead worship on that first evening in the Showering Pavilion at the showground, no one could have predicted the effect and longevity of New Wine.

The evangelist J John was one of the speakers at that first gathering from 7 to 13 August 1989. He has clear memories of the New Wine gatherings, starting with that first one:

> My wife Killy and I and our young children arrived at the first New Wine with much expectation and anticipation and it felt like 'New Wine' – the presence and peace of the Lord was tangible. New Wine deposited a grace in the lives of thousands of people and hundreds of church leaders that I am sure made a difference in their own lives and therefore made us more effective and fruitful in ministry.[8]

The Showering Pavilion, New Wine '89

Andy Park and Bryn Haworth leading Late Night Worship, New Wine '89

Despite some strong winds damaging a few of the marquees, Margaret Maynard-Madley remembers the first gathering with fondness – and with a degree of stress!

> During the last weeks leading up to the event I managed on three to four hours' sleep most nights. I felt a huge responsibility for the event. For many families it was their annual holiday! It was an expensive outlay for many, especially families. It needed to be a time of enjoyment and relaxation as well as building up spiritually. The Church needed challenging, renewing and training in the ministry of the Holy Spirit. Would the Lord 'show up' and do amazing things as we had been seeing? My mind was buzzing with all the many activities planned and the coordination of it all.

But the Lord did show up. And that first New Wine gathering was an undoubted success on every level.

CHILDREN'S WORK

One of the more obvious successes from the outset was the children's work. The children, aged from 5 to 11, were led by Captain Alan Price. There was a powerful Holy Spirit dynamic among them.

Imagine the parents arriving to collect their children from the separate building after the end of the main meeting. Imagine those parents not being able to see their children.

A moment of panic.

And then the realization of what has happened.

As the parents walk into the building, before them are hundreds of children. All of them quiet. All of them lying on the carpet, being ministered to by the Holy Spirit. Some with hands raised, some quietly praising God.

It's a picture Alan Price remembers to this day:

> Children were just in the Spirit, lying on the floor and long
> after the meeting. We didn't want to spoil it for them but
> we had to say, 'Come on, children, you need to get to bed.'
> Parents were getting a little anxious – hovering.[9]

Alan recalls one of the early years at New Wine as the year the
angels came. He didn't see any angels himself, but the children
did. A number came to him after the meeting, each saying the
same thing, each separately from the others. And each having seen
the same. Alan recalls:

> Several children came to me saying the same thing: 'Did
> you see the angels on the stage with you, Captain Alan?
> There were three of them. One of them was very big and
> had a coloured armoured plate on his chest and he was
> standing right behind you.' I tell you, I was crying. It was
> extraordinary.

Alan emphasizes the need to remember that they are still children,
and with that goes a mix of responding to the Holy Spirit,
laughing and joking together – and then fighting one another, all
in the same meeting! The carpet that was used that evening as the
children lay in God's presence was gradually shredded by them as
they sat on it and pulled its threads, so that it became smaller and
smaller each day!

In another of the early years, Alan arranged for all of the
children – the Captain's Crew as they were called – to march into
the main adults' meeting in the evening, to the surprise of those
gathered. The children were invited to pray over the adults. They
had been learning in their own sessions how to pray – how to have
one hand raised to the heavens and one hand on the person they

Captain's Crew, led by Captain Alan Price, New Wine '89

were praying for. There were a number of testimonies that night from adults who received God's healing as those children prayed.

INVESTING IN THE TEAM

New Wine wanted to ensure that what was taught and presented could be replicated in a local setting. One of the best ways to do this was to ensure that the members of the volunteer team were encouraged. Alan comments:

> The key thing is that we wanted the best for children, and more people investing in children's ministry. So we wanted to invest in the team. We sought to give the team the best experience they could have. Not just in terms of training the children but for themselves. So we really sorted out the worship we had for ourselves each morning. One afternoon, the team members came and they had their worship and asked to receive ministry. And we thought that if we invested

> heavily in the team, the children would get the overspill and I think that was one of the things we saw. We knew that that filtered out to the churches . . . We were trying to model things at a local level and not just this dynamic meeting thing.

Alan is quick to acknowledge that any success with the children in those early gatherings was very much due to the team he had with him. The children's meetings were such a success that there was a demand for cassette tapes of their worship. In addition, Alan wrote a book relating some of the things God had been doing in the meetings and helping others to learn how to lead in a similar way.[10]

After 14 years of ministry at New Wine, Alan stepped down. But to this day, he still gets letters from those who attended during that time – many of them the children he ministered to, now adults.

> It's just so exciting. We wanted the best for children. We were not babysitting. They were not second-class citizens – they deserve the best. We always said, each year, that what we were doing would not just be seen in New Wine but it would be seen in the years to come, when these children are leaders and parents themselves. That was the prophetic word. And we got to see that.

A whole generation of people has grown up in these conferences, many of whom met the Lord in ways that have dramatically shaped their lives and ministries. The children's work and youth work at New Wine has continued to be built on those values. In 2018 almost 7,000 children and young people attended the summer gatherings, with hundreds of them coming to faith for the first time.

Boulder Gang, a children's group for 10-11-year-olds,
New Wine '89

AFTER-EFFECT

The amount of post arriving at St Andrew's directly after the first
gathering was immense. People were writing from all over the
country, thanking David and Barry for their hosting of the event
and requesting that it should be the first of many.

David expressed that it had been a 'dream come true',[11] but
that didn't mean there should automatically be another event:
'It's so easy to assume that because something has been a success
once, it must be repeated. We need the guidance of God's Holy
Spirit.'[12]

The Holy Spirit did guide – and New Wine became an
annual event. As the administration grew, Margaret Maynard-
Madley's dining room was exchanged for a second-hand caravan
on the vicarage drive.

Over the years, New Wine has attracted its fair share of newspaper headlines. One of the best must be from *The Independent* in 2009, when it declared that New Wine was 'Glastonbury for God'! The paper went on to say: 'As the leaders of Britain's more mainstream denominations scratch their heads and debate how to revitalise their congregations, evangelical Christianity in Britain is going from strength to strength.'[13]

David Pytches recalls the number of healings at the New Wine gatherings as one of the highlights:

> One bricklayer had been out of work for months with agonizing pain in his wrists. He discovered his wrists were clearly healed when he tried moving them about the next morning after prayer the previous night and found the movement free and painless. People [at New Wine] were healed of whiplash, skiing problems, muscle problems, gynaecological problems, lumps on the breast, cysts on the ovaries, marriage problems – and lots of couples who could not conceive were prayed for and came back the next year with babies! There were people with hearing problems, seeing problems, sleeping problems, skin problems. I remember a man [who] begged us to pray for his twelve-year-old son at home who was covered in eczema. The next year, he told me his son had been healed that very same day and had been kept completely clear the whole year through. Hundreds received fresh fillings of the Holy Spirit, fresh anointings, new callings and giftings. For all these blessings we gave (and still give) all the glory to God.[14]

In addition to the many healings, salvations and Holy Spirit interventions, the event grew in size too. In 1993 numbers peaked at 9,000, but this proved to be too many to manage, so a limit of approximately 7,300 was set for future years.[15] When John Wimber spoke at the gathering in 1995, there were 7,500 on site and a further 1,000 in an overflow conference. That same year, the youth conference, 'Soul Survivor', brought in another 7,000 over two weeks.

The evangelist J John recalls another aspect of the New Wine gatherings. He was grateful for the worship and friendships and was particularly excited by the response to evangelism training. He regularly spoke on evangelism at the yearly gatherings and was delighted to see an attendance beyond 800 at many of them. For J John, this highlights a zeal within New Wine for all God wanted to do in the nation.

The equipping for ministry was often reflected in the work of the Holy Spirit in worship. On one of the evenings, the Holy Spirit moved in a particularly powerful way. Barry Kissell recalls what happened:

> We used to stay in a farmhouse. In between sessions I would go out to pray. On a prayer walk, I saw a vision of an incredible carpet across the valley. That evening, as we ministered, I saw it at the back of the building. It fell down on people and then unrolled forward over all the people. As it did, people began to cry out to the Lord, fall down and have incredible experience of the Spirit; those at the front didn't know what was happening. I told them to turn back and see what God was doing; it continued to roll forward, right to the front. People went forward spontaneously for prayer and were filled with the Spirit.

There were many manifestations of the Spirit in the early years of summer gatherings. Mary Kissell recalls that this experience was a year or two before the nationwide Holy Spirit outpouring which came across from Toronto in 1994. It was as if those present were getting a preview of what God was going to do in his Church.

On another prayer walk, Mary saw an incredible waterfall; then rivers; then lakes and springs; water in all its forms. She heard the Lord speak to her: 'I am refreshing my Church.' There is no doubt that this is what God did by the Holy Spirit at those early gatherings, and has continued to do since.

New Wine in the early days was booked up most years by the January before the summer. Clearly there was a need for expansion in the summer event, but also for the year-round work to develop further. Through the years, though, the summer gatherings have remained incredibly special times of encounter and celebration. New Wine's summer gatherings, now called 'United', continue to attract over 20,000 people each year, and with the move to Peterborough there is room for continued growth. Since New Wine began, hundreds of thousands have been through the gates at Shepton Mallet and its other summer events. This is all testimony to God's blessing, and vindication of those first steps of faith.

5   Developing

John and Anne Coles describe the development of New Wine beyond the summer gathering and into the churches, the community and the nation.

When David Pytches retired from leading St Andrew's in 1997, he also stepped down from his leadership of New Wine. David invited a group of other church leaders who had already been involved in New Wine for a few years to develop the work further.

There were a good number fully committed to New Wine by now, and John Coles found himself working particularly closely with Mark Melluish and Bruce Collins. As John began to lead the team, Mark took on the oversight of the summer conferences, with Bruce concentrating on the international development of New Wine.

All the leaders remained committed to developing their local churches while maintaining an outward focus with the same generosity of spirit that David had modelled. 'Don't forget,' said David, 'if the Lord blesses you, make sure you give the blessing away to others.'[1]

The team members realized that what God had begun through David and Mary could and should be developed much further. They found that many churches were asking for help. As a consequence, and as a result of a prophetic word spoken to Bruce Collins and reiterated at a leaders' day at Chorleywood, we felt we had heard from the Lord about developing a network of New Wine churches. The first Networks Manager was John Knight, who worked from a temporary building in the grounds of St Barnabas Church, Woodside Park.

CARRYING ON

The new team also needed to make a decision on the continuation of the New Wine summer conferences. It wasn't a hard decision, though.

All the churches were benefiting from their members attending the summer gatherings and returning with a fresh vision of God, a fresh vision of what church could be, and a fresh

John and Anne Coles, New Wine 2016

understanding of how to make Jesus known to their friends and neighbours. And the team members' own children were among them! They couldn't let New Wine finish because they, their families and their churches would be impoverished if they did.

Anne Coles recalls:

> Every year we would set off for the summer New Wine festival with a car-full of four children and all the kit to camp for one or two weeks; the journey might have been long, sometimes with horrendous traffic jams, but nothing could overshadow the whoops of joy and screams of excitement from the back of the car as we drove over the top of the hill above the showground and saw the tents and caravans below us. It was as if all their dreams had come true at once! Such was the New Wine effect on our children!

Abi Figuero, John and Anne's daughter, dates the start of her call to work as a missionary to her early experiences of New Wine:

> I started going to New Wine when I was nine years old and every year I would wander around the marketplace. The colour and variety of the work of God around the world attracted me. I started sponsoring a child in Colombia through Compassion. A few years later I went on a trip to Colombia with Christian Solidarity Worldwide and eventually became a missionary with Latin Link in Colombia. All those contacts came from the marketplace, and my passion to serve in the kingdom of God came from years of spiritual formation and living examples I saw modelled in the youth groups and leadership.

Financing the conferences was an issue, though. The team members negotiated with their parish church councils over their churches' commitment of time and money to a vision beyond the parish and local community. It was important that each church not only believed in giving at least a tithe of its income to mission but was also willing to give a tithe of its leader's time and energy to the wider Church.

VOLUNTEERS

From the beginning of the summer gatherings, a large number of volunteers were needed. These people came from local churches that shared the vision and values of New Wine, and had learned that 'you grow by giving'. In gratitude for God's work in their lives they gave up part of their summer holiday to serve God, and always reported that they were greatly blessed in return – coming to serve year after year.

They also found that the New Wine conferences, because of the intentional link between the summer and ongoing local work throughout the year, were wonderful places to train and develop skills. Canny church leaders have come to realize that if they want to train someone in children's or youth work, they should bring that person as a volunteer for a week-long full-on immersion in serving on a kids' or youth team. Canny older teenagers realize that they can get a free place at New Wine and learn all kinds of useful skills if they are volunteers!

In 2018 about 3,800 volunteers served over the two weeks. The catering tent now serves 1,200 meals every lunchtime, plus breakfast and dinner. All the infrastructure to support the conference has had to grow as the conference has grown, but the fundamental truth remains – New Wine's summer conference is put on by local churches for local churches.

COMMUNITY AND SOCIAL TRANSFORMATION

Mark Melluish was working with a strapline for his church at St Paul's Ealing: 'A church in the community for the community'. He brought the same emphasis to the summer conference by developing a wider range of daytime cafés, after-hours entertainment, and youth and children's activities.

The summer gatherings became much better at offering a holiday alongside the conference sessions; for families who had been attending for a number of years this was very attractive. Additionally, Mark and his wife Lindsay pioneered seminars on Christian parenting, and in the course of it wrote a book, *Family Time*,[2] which presented a practical model for parents on how to raise their children as believers. They were also using it as a course that could run for believers and not-yet believers; New Wine wanted to model things in the summer that could be multiplied throughout the country in any church and in any context.

Mark was also committed to social transformation, and his involvement with Tearfund (he was a member of its board) meant that he was well connected with the world of Christian development agencies. He introduced significant streams of seminars dedicated to helping people grapple with the issues of poverty, relief and development. At his suggestion the summer conference began to have two offerings – one dedicated to some aspect of world mission, and the other dedicated to a number of projects that were supported around the UK (or the world) by Network churches.

THE PROPHETIC

Bruce Collins' passion was the prophetic, which 'prepares the way for the Lord'.[3] He was in effect developing a school of highly gifted prophetic people. When he saw some of those whom he had taught and trained growing in the accuracy and significance of the revelation they were receiving, he gave them further opportunities. He took them with him to minister to church leaders and on various courses. They were heavily involved in the prayer ministry at all the summer conferences, and Bruce's teaching sessions on hearing the voice of God in the prophetic were some of the essential building blocks of the summer conference programme.

EVERY MEMBER A MINISTER

John Coles' local emphasis tended to be in training every member of his church to minister confidently in the power of the Spirit wherever he or she might be, rather than just within the church building. He frequently taught on healing, trained the ministry teams for the summer conferences, and also wrote the New Wine resource book originally called *Developing a Healing Ministry* and then later *Learning to Heal*.[4]

When John heard about Healing on the Streets in 2005, as developed by Causeway Coast Vineyard church, he was quick to find out more and then introduce it to the Network at the National Leadership conference in Harrogate. David Pytches had always said, 'The meeting place is the training place for the marketplace', but now he was asking, 'Have we really taken Jesus' ministry to the sick on to the streets and into the marketplace?' So John visited David McClay, the vicar of Willowfields, Belfast, to see how he and the church members had put this into practice in their parish. On a very wet Saturday morning they took up their stance on the pavement of one of the streets through East Belfast and waited . . . Eventually, despite the rain, they ended up praying for a number of people, who had some measure of healing, but all were touched by the love of God and extremely grateful to him. John felt this was a model that New Wine churches could follow, so he introduced it to the Network at the National Leadership conference in Harrogate, providing each participant with a teaching CD on how to implement it. This quickly became part of the ministry for churches in towns and cities around the UK, normally initiated by New Wine Network churches, and usually in collaboration with other local churches. Often this healing ministry attracted broken and isolated individuals, and subsequently led to the establishing of night shelters, food banks, street pastors, and other mercy ministries.

John and Anne also developed the seminar 'Making More of Marriage', which then became a book of the same title.[5] One of the earliest attendees at their seminars, Catherine Hill, developed this seminar further, along with her husband. Catherine has subsequently taken on a role of national significance as UK Director of Care for the Family. Marriage enrichment seminars have remained a significant element of the summer seminar programme.

YOUTH AND CHILDREN

The youth and older children were gathered in their own meetings such as Rock Solid, Club One, and Thirst. This work had initially been led by Mike Pilavachi, and because it grew at such a rate it was clear that a new conference for teenagers was needed: this was how Soul Survivor was born. 'They made so much noise late at night that the families were glad when they left,' David Pytches jokingly said.

Youth and children's work remained a staple part of the main summer conferences, though, and by defining a clear vision and values, and recruiting leaders for each age group who were practitioners in their local New Wine Network churches, this ministry continues to grow.

A visitor to New Wine in 2018, who had not attended for 15 years, remarked that it was 'amazing to see the youth work being led with the same vision and values that were here fifteen years ago, but with a completely different group of leaders in charge'. By God's grace, the baton is being passed to the next generation.

Around 2005 a Chinese house-church leader came as an invited speaker. She was shown the whole site, observing families having fun together, and then the venues where age-appropriate worship teaching and prayer ministry was happening. Seeing the obvious participation and enjoyment of children and adults together, she commented: 'In China this is what we imagine heaven will be like.'

LAKESIDE

The original week-long summer conference was soon not big enough to supply the demand for places, and consequently a weekend conference, called Lakeside, was born. This shorter event, held by the lake at the end of the Royal Bath and West Showground, was helpful in introducing the ethos of New Wine to people who may not have felt ready to commit to a full week's event.

The Soul Survivor conference was held on the remaining larger portion of the site at the same time. For some it meant that they could come as a family to the showground, with the teenage

A weekend conference named Lakeside, held at the Bath and West
Showground

John Coles leading a seminar at Lakeside Conference 1997

children taking part in Soul Survivor while the adults were at Lakeside. Some moved on from the weekend to the full week, but others preferred the more intimate environment of the 1,500 Lakeside delegates.

Lakeside wasn't really financially viable and Soul Survivor wanted to expand to fill the whole site, so the team agreed to move on from Lakeside and have two full weeks of summer conferences. This meant that more leaders would have to take on more significant roles. Mark and Lindsay Melluish led one of the weeks, and Mark and Karen Bailey began to lead the other. They also began to involve Charlie and Anita Cleverly, from St Aldate's Oxford, who had a heart for intercession. Charlie and Anita were willing to help create a venue at the summer conferences dedicated to seminars on worship, intercession and intimacy with the Lord. The 'Hungry' venue, as it became known, became a favourite for many over the decade they ran it, and the lives of many were transformed both in that tent and through the Lord answering prayers first expressed in that venue.

SUPPORTING LEADERS

As the New Wine work grew, operations were moved into one location managed by Phil George. There was also a need to develop training, and the leadership team began to work with Westminster Theological Centre. They identified that the theological teaching the centre provided was set in the context of worship and prayer ministry; this embodied New Wine's understanding of Scripture, the ministry of the Spirit, and the advance of the kingdom of God. It proved to be a good match. New Wine financially enabled the development and delivery of this training through a number of hubs based in New Wine churches around the country, and although Westminster Theological Centre now works independently, New Wine believes the centre remains a key resource, providing a high-quality training track for many growing leaders.

New Wine also provided considerable leadership training directly through its annual Leadership Conference, starting out at the High Leigh Conference Centre in Hertfordshire and, after a few other locations, ending up at the Harrogate International Conference Centre. Most of the early speakers were senior pastors in Vineyard churches in the USA, and built on the legacy of John Wimber and his friendship with David Pytches. When Bill Johnson, Senior Pastor of Bethel Church, Redding, California, spoke at the Leadership Conference in 2007, the numbers peaked at around 1,950, with many people who weren't part of New Wine coming to hear him.

As numbers and the Network have continued to grow, the leaders' conferences have moved into regions, alternating biannually with the larger Harrogate conference.

In addition, over the years, New Wine has facilitated leaders' retreats. These provide a place where church leaders can find fresh faith, vision and hope. In the early days, these were held at Teddy and Margaret Saunders' house, 'The Hensol', in Chorleywood, so were often referred to as 'Hensol Retreats'. As the network grew, these leaders' retreats were held in a number of different New Wine churches across the country.

As well as receiving the practical teaching, each leader was immersed in a group of leaders with similar values, with a focus on hearing the voice of the Lord. It was this focus on personal prophetic prayer ministry that signified that the retreats expected the Lord to reveal himself to participants, to soak them in his love, and to establish them in their calling and empower them with his Spirit.

One such leader said:

> I was delighted when on the first day someone prayed for me personally and prophetically – it was the first time that had happened in a long while. Then to my utter surprise it happened again the next day, and continued every day throughout the week. I went home enormously refreshed and determined to ask people to pray for me in the same way in the future.

FURTHER TRAINING

One of the most common questions asked by leaders was: 'How do I develop *that* ministry in *my* church?' In response, John Coles began to develop training days on healing, with Bruce Collins doing the same for the subject of prophecy.

They then trained a number of other trainers in these ministries who delivered the training on Saturdays around the Network, at the request of Network leaders. The vision was to make the training as local as possible, to ensure it was as accessible to as many people as possible. Individual churches were encouraged to invite other churches to join them, consequently not only increasing the number of churches delivering that ministry but also further strengthening links between churches around the country. Many people trained on these days, then became involved in prayer ministry at the summer conferences.

More recently, 'Third Person' training days led by John Peters, and 'Walking on Water' training days led by Paul and Becky Harcourt, have been developed. These cover similar ground but with a slightly different perspective and emphasis.

In order to meet different needs, annual 'retreats' for different leadership groups were developed: one for rural and village church leaders, another for urban and estate church leaders, with occasional gatherings for leaders of larger churches. Ministry heads have now been appointed for each of these groups, with the responsibility of ensuring the best possible support for leaders in these environments. A church planters' network has been established for the same reason.

WOMEN'S MINISTRY

Anne Coles writes:

> The Lord gloriously filled John and me with his Spirit separately but on the same Easter weekend in 1983, when we were both tired and disappointed with ministry in our first church. Just when we felt we were failing the Lord, he lovingly took over and showed us how he builds the Church and graciously involves us! John and I had been side by side, as it were, learning from the Lord. As Peter pointed out at the first Pentecost, God had promised to pour out his Spirit on all people: 'Your sons and daughters will prophesy' (Acts 2.17), and we had seen the Lord use men and women without respect to their gender.

It was during the summer of 2000, as Anne was sitting praying by the swimming pool on holiday in France, when the Lord seemed to say to her that at the turn of the century she was to 'Go home and gather the women'. Anne was surprised. However, in obedience to the command, she invited women to the first New Wine women's day in 2001 with a vision to see them filled and equipped by the Holy Spirit. John and Anne quickly discovered that women in churches up and down the country were being involved in practical ministry but were often unaware of the spiritual power that was available to them and were unsure how to walk in it. At its height, there were over 2,500 women at the main London event.

It soon became clear that the wives of church leaders were also a neglected part of the Church, so the first of many annual retreats for them was held in 2002. Healing prayer ministry was an essential element of those times, as many expressed the pain and disappointment of standing alongside their spouses in ministry. Anne felt the retreats provided a safe place where these women could be open about their feelings among their peers.

In 1994 the first women were ordained into the Anglican Church, and by the end of the century there were now a growing number of such ordained women coming to New Wine events. The question was asked: was New Wine going to welcome the leadership of women? Through teaching seminars in the summer and the first conference for women in leadership in 2004, the New Wine leadership began to understand, honour and encourage, and support and promote these women. John has been delighted to be asked to write references for women considering ordination, and for those becoming vicars and archdeacons, and has now recruited Bishop Jill Duff as a New Wine trustee.

By 2011 there was a growing army of women released into places of influence in the Church and the marketplace. A series of annual conferences in the three different regions of the country – North, Central/South West, London/South East – were held to inspire and encourage women. These gatherings were addressed by women who were involved both in ministry at ground level and in refining their speaking gifts.

The National Women's Day has provided a significant benefit to the Network, as well as a number of lower-key women's retreats. Women would pray prophetically for one another at these retreats, as well as seeing the Lord heal and minister deeply.

Loneliness in leadership can wear many down. Through the Network there are different opportunities not only for inspiration through good teaching but also for transformation through worship and prayer ministry, all applied to the local setting.

New Wine is much more than a summer gathering.

6 Growing

John and Anne Coles continue to tell New Wine's story as it begins to have an impact on the nation.

Just before John Wimber died, he recommended to David Pytches a book relating to church development by Christian Schwarz.[1] This is an extensive scientific study on what makes churches healthy and therefore grow. David circulated a copy of this book to the New Wine leaders, and they worked with these principles for a number of years.

It's probably true to say that the leaders of New Wine were not interested so much in the growth of numbers as in being filled with the Holy Spirit – knowing that as a consequence of that, there would be growth. There has, though, been a good growth in numbers and a significant impact on many towns and cities in the UK. *The Road to Growth*, Bob Jackson's influential book on church growth in the Church of England, specifically highlighted the New Wine Network as being worthy of study:

> It can be seen that many of the New Wine values embrace features identified in this book as being good for growth, for example, worship centred on encounter with God, relational community for all ages, church planting. Moreover, the

context of the values and vision appears to be that of a
church-in-mission in a non-Christian culture.[2]

Directly or indirectly, many ministers have been encouraged
by New Wine, through both the summer conferences and the
year-round local networks. Among that number would be Justin
Welby, the current Archbishop of Canterbury, who was a regular
attender at New Wine with his church and family for 12 years
when he was working in the Coventry diocese.

GOING NORTH

By 2002 the conferences at Shepton Mallet were reaching capacity.
This capacity had been gradually increasing from 7,500 to 11,500
as New Wine helped to build the infrastructure of the site; that's a
nice way of saying that New Wine helped with improvements in
water supply, and most especially in sewage removal! At a leaders'
meeting someone said, 'How about doing one further north?'
The seeds of New Wine North had been planted. Ian and Nadine
Parkinson from All Saints' Marple, just outside Manchester, were
invited to lead. Over 60 church leaders gathered with Ian and
Nadine to discuss with John Coles the possibility of such a week.
The first New Wine North was in 2005 at Harrogate Showground
and filled it to its capacity of 3,000 the very first year; it then
moved to the larger showground at Newark for future years.
Attendance quickly grew to around 7,000 a year. Each venue on
site had a team whose members took responsibility for setting the
culture of that venue and modelling the ministry of the Spirit.
The significance of this was made clear with the realization in
2007 that the gathering was attracting a significant number from
non-book cultures – people who didn't have a typical middle-class
approach to learning. Consequently, Ian and Nadine made plans

for a new venue, 'Impact', which would be dedicated to empowering people for mission and ministry particularly in urban areas of the northern cities in England. One bishop commented that this was 'the best sign of hope for urban mission that he had seen in the Church of England for years'.[3]

Ian began to mentor some younger church leaders, and in doing so became aware of the lack of provision for young adults, and the lack of opportunity for them to lead their own peers at the summer conferences. So he invited Luke Smith from Fusion to dream and to present a venue dedicated to such people. As a result, 'Burn' became a fantastic training ground for young adults in leadership.

Another innovation pioneered by Ian and Nadine was a 'school of ministry' approach which gave delegates the chance

Matthew Porter and Mark Carey leading a session at
New Wine North

to book places in a series of seminars for the week with intensive learning rather than just picking and choosing individual seminars. The schools included teaching on leadership, prophecy, evangelism, and Christians in the workplace. These schools became a model for the more definite 'streaming' of seminars that has characterized New Wine summer gatherings ever since.

Logistics and cost constraints meant that eventually the northern gathering had to close and it was brought back together under a 'United' label in 2014 at Shepton Mallet. By introducing a long weekend conference in Thirsk and with the decision to move more centrally in the UK to Peterborough for 2018 onwards, the loss for those who attended the northern gathering has been lessened.

The two summer conferences in Shepton Mallet had become 'regionalized' for a number of years. Mark and Karen Bailey led one for the Central and South West Region, and Mark and Lindsay Melluish led another for the London and South East Region; both had involved and trained significant new leaders from their regions. This regionalization ended in 2014 when the three conferences merged and became the new 'United' gathering.

Aerial photo of Bath and West Showground during New Wine 2016

VENUES 2 AND 3

In 2005 a new second venue for adults was launched at Shepton Mallet, called simply Venue 2. Led by John and Debby Wright, it had its own programme of morning and evening sessions, with the same basic ingredients of teaching, worship and ministry as the main meeting in the Big Top. But it cultivated a very relaxed, informal feel, with cafés open throughout the day, including during meetings.

In the evenings a bar was opened and various types of fun entertainment were held there. Among the evening entertainment was a speed-dating night. Several couples started their relationship as a result of meeting on one of those nights!

In later years, a third venue was opened. The team was learning that involvement leads to commitment. By increasing the number of venues, there was an increase in the opportunities for church leaders to be significantly involved and consequentially become more committed to New Wine vision and values throughout the year.

FULL-TIME LEADERSHIP

In 2005 it became clear to John Coles that the demands of leading St Barnabas as well as overseeing the continuing growth of New Wine were too much. The church now had a Sunday attendance of around 600, with a large staff team, and had planted four other churches, together with supporting 15 missionaries around the world. John had appointed Henry Kendal as his associate in 1999 and it was Henry who was appointed as John's successor in 2006. John was then employed to lead New Wine full time.

This change probably came slightly too late since, just after Christmas 2006, John suffered a heart attack. Anne had had a significant dream the previous evening in which she knew the Lord was asking her to pray as she had never prayed before. She was out of the house when the heart attack began and returned to discover paramedics attending John; they had been called by their daughter Abi, who realized the severity of what John was experiencing. Anne immediately began to pray with Abi and with Simon, one of their sons who was at home. They prayed incessantly over the next three hours. The medics used their defibrillator ('That's the first time I've ever used one – I'm glad it worked,' said the paramedic. 'And so am I,' said Anne). John was 'blue-lighted' to hospital and had a stent fitted in the offending artery. His high cholesterol level was the underlying reason for the attack, but the doctors also suggested that stress would have contributed to the attack. By God's grace and medical care John was given another life in which to serve the Lord. It became clear to everyone that he needed to say 'no' more frequently and ensure that he handed on greater responsibility to others.

John discovered there were advantages and disadvantages to being employed full time by New Wine. He was able to give more time to Network leaders, to working with Phil George on leading the staff team, to thinking strategically about the development of New Wine, and to giving his time to new projects. But there were downsides too. There appeared to be a loss of credibility with the leaders of the larger churches, who fairly quickly realized he was no longer a peer facing the same issues. However, when John planted a house church he gained fresh credibility, especially with leaders of smaller churches with limited resources. It also went some way to addressing the criticism that the team was only presenting the idea of 'big is beautiful'.

Subsequently both Mark Bailey, who was National Leader from 2014 to 2016, and Paul Harcourt, who has led from 2016 onwards, chose to stay in the leadership of their churches as well as lead New Wine. 'New Wine is a network of practitioners, and I must remain a practitioner,' Paul said. However, his development of the National Leadership Team has created space for leaders of various sizes and contexts of church to become involved in strategic decision-making.

IDENTITY

As this book explains, the name New Wine was primarily chosen to rhyme with the year New Wine started – '89. But its suitability also lies in the biblical imagery of the word 'wine', and the concept of 'wineskins'. When Jesus spoke about the need to put new wine into new wineskins, he was indicating that when people were filled with the Spirit they would find that they could no longer fit their thinking and living into their previous life-shapes or church-shapes; a radical reorientation would be required.

The members of a leadership team, meeting in 2010, were trying to complete a 'branding' review and were searching for a strapline to encapsulate the mission. On a flip chart was a whole range of ideas. Then, almost as if prompted by the Spirit, the focus became the local church, and the vision became changing the nations. 'Local churches changing nations' was quickly adopted. This also gave fresh emphasis to the role that local networks played as leaders took their churches into renewal. Bob Jackson noted in his research that, 'This sharing of ideas and stories is one of the main functions of the New Wine Network, and probably one of the main reasons why churches whose clergy belong to that network tend to grow.'[4]

At the same time, John rewrote the vision statement, encapsulating the statement 'To see the nation changed'. The intention was to ensure that the vision didn't just focus on the encounter that individuals had with God but also on churches built on those same values. Additionally, for the first time the team included a vision for church planting which, although owned and practised by some, had not really been corporately owned, planned or celebrated:

> To see churches
> renewed, strengthened and planted,
> living out the word of God in every aspect of life,
> serving God by reaching
> the lost, broken and poor,
> and demonstrating the good news of the kingdom of God
> to all.

GENERATIONS

The promise of the outpouring of the Spirit in Joel 2 was fulfilled at Pentecost (Acts 2) and was for all – men and women, young and old, sons and daughters. This is a key truth for New Wine and is reflected in introducing children and youth to the fullness of life in the Spirit as much as it does with adult delegates at conferences and gatherings. 'Learning by doing' is a major emphasis – for all ages. One leader was led to comment: 'Of all the Christian conferences I have been at, New Wine is the one that seems to value and promote working with children and youth as much as with adults.'

The New Wine Discipleship Year was introduced in 2011. The year includes a practical internship in particular areas of church life (youth, children, media, administration, ministry to the poor, and so on) as well as a good biblical and theological unit, based on modules. By 2019 the number of students who had completed the Discipleship Year was 700, and the programme continues to grow.

LEADERSHIP SUCCESSION

At various points in the development of New Wine, the radical question has been asked: 'Lord, do you want New Wine to continue?'

Following a particularly difficult time in the leadership team during 2016, two consultation groups were created. One was a group of New Wine-friendly church leaders from other streams of Charismatic renewal, all of whom had significant input to New Wine's story. Their initial conclusion was: 'Keep going.' Second, they reflected on the need to empower and profile a younger generation of leaders, and the need to not lose focus.

Their third observation – that New Wine was really a family network rather than a movement – caused significant discussion. For some time, there had been the language of 'movement'. We wanted to ensure that our network was empowering and intentional about making a difference. However, the truth was that New Wine was not one single movement and didn't want to be as prescriptive as some other 'movements'.

The second group consulted was made up of a selection of leaders within New Wine who had a very diverse variety of experience, responsibility, geography and longevity. The discussion with this group revealed that New Wine was not 'owned' by a small leadership group that could choose to close it down. Its vision and values, and the nature of its events, were now so embodied in and shared by so many that if the Leadership Team had chosen to stop New Wine's activities, others would have started them again!

With Paul Harcourt's appointment as National Leader, there was a clear brief to develop a new, younger and more diverse leadership team. This is always a work in progress, but the development of the National Leadership Team bears this out.

7 Soul Survivor

Mike Pilavachi celebrates all that God has done through the Soul Survivor gatherings.[1]

'Mike, do you have a moment?'

It was just after the evening service at St Andrew's Chorleywood. I was the very new (and very green) youth leader. So when the vicar of the parish asks to see you, it can set your mind racing. What had I done wrong? I'd contributed to the service – had I said something I shouldn't have? It wouldn't have been the first time. I had a track record of engaging mouth before brain!

As we found a quiet corner at the back of the room, David looked at me with a frown on his face. Here it comes, I thought. I'm about to be the youth leader with the shortest employment record in the history of St Andrew's!

But I needn't have worried.

'Mike, I wonder whether you could start joining us in our leaders' meetings? I think you'll have something to contribute, and it would be good for you to see more of what we're doing and discussing.'

Wow. He really was taking a risk with me. I was shocked. And delighted.

LEADERS' MEETINGS

So there we were. David and Mary Pytches. Richard and Prue Bedwell. Barry Kissell. All sorts of other people who had been there for years. And me. I was the totally junior member of staff, having arrived as youth leader in 1987. Needless to say, I was feeling out of my depth.

But David was great. He believed in me. I learned so much in those meetings. It was a great time. A leadership learning curve.

It wasn't long before we were discussing something that became a central part of our lives.

'It's OK having all these leadership conferences,' David said. 'And I do appreciate all God is doing by his Holy Spirit in those times. But they are just for leaders. What about our congregations? When John Wimber was with us, one of his main points was that healing was for everyone. The baptism in the Spirit is for all of us. John used to say, "Everybody gets to play." But the way we do things at the moment, only the leaders get to play!'

We talked some more. Some of the leaders had visited a Bible Week that summer.

'What if we were to do something like a Bible Week? What if we had a gathering for everybody? Is it possible? Could we do it? Could we afford it?'

The more we talked, the more we knew: God was on our case. We didn't have a name at that stage, but New Wine had been born in our hearts in a leaders' meeting.

We came up with the name one day when out walking. It's funny that so many of us have been putting a spiritual spin on it all these years, that it's all about needing new wineskins and it's all about the transformation – but the real reason was that it rhymed! But of course, it became much more than a rhyme.

Mike Pilavachi

The administration for that gathering was run from a caravan in the vicarage drive with a wire from David and Mary's house providing electricity for the caravan, and for the first years that was the hub. Jeannie Morgan helped Margaret Maynard-Madley with the administration. I was in and out, working on the youth. And that was it. That was the team.

HEADING UP THE YOUTH

I was asked to head up the youth aspects of the gathering from that very first year. It was an increase in numbers from the St Andrew's youth group, but that first year it wasn't too big compared to how it developed later. I was able to step up by degrees as the event grew.

In 1989 there were around 300 youth. We met in an old abattoir on the Shepton Mallet site. I remember it had a sloping floor which caused some concerns when we wanted to set up a stage.

Looking back now, what we did was unbelievably basic. A few worship songs. A bit of a preach. We just met in the mornings, with the youth joining the main congregation in the evenings.

But it worked. So much so, I found that other churches were inviting me to go and speak to their youth groups, and to help them run youth weekends.

A year or so later, we started doing something called 'New Wine at Wycliffe', which was a weekend youth event. We used the Wycliffe Bible Translators premises near High Wycombe. People came from different churches – and from other denominations too. We were learning all the time. But clearly, God had his hand on it all.

It was about that time that a few of us began to dream.

THE START

Numbers at New Wine Youth were growing rapidly by now. With the experience of the Wycliffe weekends, a team of us began to think big. What if we took some of the best bits from other events such as Spring Harvest and Greenbelt and combined them with what we were already doing with New Wine Youth? What if we took ourselves a bit less seriously; provided some entertainment as well as worship; offered something that would be attractive to youth that were not from a church background? How about a café? What if we had a bit of fun too? What if . . .?

I couldn't get the ideas out of my head. I knew it was absolutely impossible. Being involved with the administration, I knew the costs. To put on a separate event from New Wine would not be cost effective.

But still the ideas wouldn't go away . . .

I decided to go and talk to David about it. Get it out of my system. Allow him to say 'no' in his polite but firm way, and be done with it. I would have been able to get it out of my head, and I could then leave it there.

'It sounds ridiculous to me,' said David.

A pause.

'But it sounds like it might be God. So let's have a go.'

There was no 'New Wine is not on a firm financial footing'. There was no 'You haven't thought this through'. No normal person would have said 'yes' in David's position. But there we were – with an idea and a commitment. And a lot of prayer!

We decided we would commit to it for the first time in 1993, alongside New Wine.

And we needed a new name.

THE NAME

The name for the new event was a problem. I remember asking a number of friends to help. We even had a brainstorming night. Not that our brains were stormed particularly. The best we came up with was '20/20 Vision'.

Someone suggested 'Soul Survivor'. I wasn't a fan.

'That's not going to work – it's so depressing! So our souls are just going to survive, are they? What sort of message is that going to give? Surely it should be called "Soul Thriving" or something like that?'

The name stayed with me, though.

A week later I was listening to David Parker[2] preaching at St Andrew's. I can't remember now much of what he said, but one sentence stood out then. And it still stands out today: 'For many young people today, to live in victory is simply to survive.'

That was it. Soul Survivor! We had our name. We had our vision. We wanted the youth and young adults of today to thrive, not simply to survive.

Our first Soul Survivor was in 1993. And 1,896 young people came – I counted them all myself! We had Kevin Prosch leading worship, along with a very young Matt Redman. It was amazing. Matt was still a teenager, but he had such an anointing on him. In later years he became our main worship leader at Soul Survivor.

I continued to lead the New Wine youth event as well. In fact, the year before our first Soul Survivor is etched in my memory. By now we were gathering around 1,000 young people. We were out of the abattoir, I'm glad to say. We met in a big tent. Delirious? came that year. I remember Martin Smith singing 'I Could Sing of Your Love Forever' – Delirious? sang it for the first time there. Martin kept repeating the refrain 'I could sing of your love forever' over and over. I wondered what was wrong with him. I thought he'd forgotten the next verse. Until I saw what was going on. Kids were on the floor. We just sang that line for half an hour from gentle and quiet, through to a crescendo. I thought, Something's happening here!

God met us in a wonderful way.

A FIRST-YEAR REVIEW

I had no doubts about God meeting us on that first year of Soul Survivor. But I did have big doubts as to whether there would be

One of the first Soul Survivor gatherings

a second year. The administrative challenges were fierce. Starting a new camp nearly killed the administration team. New Wine as a movement was still small. We didn't have a big team and, financially, attracting 1,896 teenagers was not going to make money either. It was draining us in every way.

David came to see me. I anticipated the worst.

'Mike, I came down to tell you that this would have to be the first and last Soul Survivor, because we can't afford it financially and it's killing the team. But I've walked around the last two days and God is here.'

I'll never forget his next words.

'Who am I to fight against God? We will carry on.'

Soul Survivor was a great cost to New Wine. It really was. That is one of the main things I wanted to say. It's an important part of the story.

Year two brought in 4,000 young people. In year three it was 6,000. By the time we reached year seven in 1999, there were 16,000 young people. It reached its peak in 2014 with 30,000 attending.

REACHING CITIES

At the early Soul Survivor events we had the privilege of listening to speakers like Tony Campolo and Jim Wallis. They made us aware in a way that was new to us that God has an agenda that reaches out to everyone in terms of both evangelism and social action. So we decided to do something about it.

In 2000 we helped lead a mission in Manchester with the Message Tribe, Youth For Christ, and Oasis. A total of 11,000 young people spent ten days in Manchester working with social action projects. The superintendent of the Greater Manchester police force noted that for the first time in his experience, there had been no crime reported in the deprived areas visited by the volunteers during the time they were there.[3]

Then in 2004 we had Soul in the City, right through London, where we worked with 776 partner churches. About 11,500 young people came and camped at three sites on the outskirts of London, and they paid to serve and work alongside the churches. It was an amazing time and helped to spark a number of social action projects.

REACHING NATIONS

Matt Redman's worship ministry was taking off and he had some incredible prophecies too, confirming that ministry. I accompanied him and encouraged him. And it was during that time that we had a number of requests for a Soul Survivor-type event in other nations. One of the most vigorous requests came from the Netherlands.

With hindsight, we were not close enough to what was going on there. We gave the name away without maintaining our input. I was very aware that I didn't want to create some kind of autocratic control, but maybe we went a bit too far the other way. Nevertheless, the Netherlands venture was a success and many young people gathered together, with lives changed as the Holy Spirit did his work.

We don't really push the Soul Survivor name now – especially as we are closing the gathering in the UK. But we still serve with all sorts of folks and different camps. It's about the values; it's not about the name.

In May 2018 we announced that, after 27 years of events, the 2019 conferences would be the last. While we knew this would come as a shock to many, we believed that God had spoken to us and this would be the right time for us to step aside and make space for others to rise up. It was not a decision we took lightly – we had been wrestling with it for a substantial amount of time.

Right from the start of Soul Survivor we had always said that when God told us to stop, we would. We believed that time had come, and we wanted to be obedient. We've always been humbled by the amount of support we've been shown, so we knew that some would feel sad about this decision. We also knew, though, that God said, 'I will build my Church' – he never said, 'I will build my Soul Survivor.' Our passion has always been to support the local church where faith is lived out as family week in and week out, not to create our own movement.

I regularly speak at Easter Camp on the north island of New Zealand, where we get 4,500 to 5,000 teenagers, which is stunning. There's a camp called Praise Camp in Switzerland which has 7,000 German-speaking youth – an incredible percentage. Then there are various other events like these in other parts of the world. God has used us to be a catalyst for a season rather than a movement. Names may change, but the Spirit has just started to do something. And that something is still flowing and still spreading out.

INTIMACY

As I reflect on what God has done, a lot can be described by the word 'intimacy'. We learned from John Wimber and the Vineyard movement that it's worshipping Jesus that is important. It's never about the preacher or the worship leader. As I write this, I can hear David Pytches' voice saying: 'Let God be God. Make space for him. Take risks. Step back!'

It's such good advice.

We believe in 'every-member ministry' – it's for everyone. It's not meant to be for special superstars. Everyone gets equipped to do it. Some have particular roles and functions, but the whole ministry of Jesus is the whole Church of Jesus. We aim to be profoundly Christian but hopefully in a very non-religious way. We communicate to the culture; we communicate to non-Christians without dumbing down what we believe. We are hopefully sensitive to only speaking for as long as the Lord wants us to in each situation. We try not to hide or manipulate anything. We're informal and relaxed. We're inclusive and not exclusive. We don't have a special language. We care for the poor and the broken, the marginalized and the dispossessed. It's part of what we're meant to be.

That's the Church I'm talking about. And by God's grace, Soul Survivor has played its part in the Church's story.

8 Worship

Worship has always been a central part of all that New Wine is about. Ralph Turner investigates its role and its development within the New Wine family.

As Matt Redman says, 'Worship is the people of God in the presence of God, pouring out the praises of God.'[1] As he reflects on worship and his own personal journey, he is grateful for all God has done. Matt's story is intertwined with the New Wine story.

THE WIMBER MEETINGS

The story of worship in New Wine goes right back to the beginning. When John Wimber first came over from the USA for those meetings at St Andrew's Chorleywood, he brought 29 other people with him. Among them were a good few worship leaders. The worship that accompanied those meetings was rather different from the regular style within the Anglican Church. David Pytches describes it as using 'simple songs we had never heard before'.[2] Their simplicity, alongside lyrics that expressed love for God, was effective in laying a foundation for the word that was then preached. Some found the songs repetitive as they were sung over and over again, with few verses. But as Charles Whitehead summarized: 'Where some complain that it's repetitive, I find the repetition of truth liberating; where others may say the words are simplistic, I *want* to be childlike before the Father.'[3]

Terry Virgo, founder of the Newfrontiers movement, was another early UK friend of John Wimber. The movement was already enjoying the Vineyard worship cassettes before John visited. Terry comments:

> The gentle worship style that came from the Vineyard was . . . immediately popular with many English charismatics . . . [though] the popular 'Hosanna' seemed to be the only up-tempo song in their repertoire . . .
>
> The Vineyard cassettes were being played everywhere. It is my conviction that charismatic renewal had been fading in the UK outside the new churches but John powerfully renewed the renewal![4]

Alongside the message and preaching of John Wimber, the worship he introduced provided a platform for that renewal.

John Wimber's intention in the worship was to pursue intimacy. The songs were almost entirely addressed to God or Jesus and brought an expectancy of meeting with the Lord.[5]

MATT REDMAN

And this is where Matt Redman rejoins the story. As a young boy, he attended those first Wimber meetings at Chorleywood:

> I was only seven at the time but I was taken along to the meeting at church. Those songs just ushered in a fresh intimacy which I'd never experienced in church worship

and music. I was really drawn to the idea that you cannot only sing to God and He hears our songs and you can bless the heart of God through songs, but there's actually another dimension where you can engage with God through songs. You can meet Him and draw near to Him through music and He draws near to you.[6]

As Matt grew, so did his ability with a guitar. But he was secretive about it, avoiding any public leading of worship. That was until Mike Pilavachi got involved.

Mike, who was Matt's youth leader at St Andrew's, tried to trick Matt into leading as often as possible. The hoaxes were often elaborate, like the time when an older worship leader just happened to bump into Matt and Mike in the church car park:

OLDER WORSHIP LEADER: [Looking worried] 'Oh, Mike – what am I to do? I am supposed to be leading worship tomorrow but my guitar has broken. Do you know anyone who could do it instead?'

MIKE PILAVACHI: 'Oh dear! What a terrible shame that is. I wonder who we could ask . . .'

[Both men turn and stare at Matt][7]

Gradually Matt's confidence grew and the need for hoaxes reduced. He threw himself into the world of worship, attending conferences and church events, and heading off on faith-sharing trips with others from St Andrew's.

The opportunities to lead grew rapidly as Matt got older – especially as St Andrew's was growing so fast in terms of numbers and meetings. Matt says:

In a more typical church you might get on the rota once a month, but at St Andrew's we had multiple services, church plants and extra meetings. I'd lead on Sunday mornings and some evenings, then there would be midweek meetings and Friday nights – so even from a young age I'd be leading four times a week. Then when I was 19 and employed by the church I could be leading up to 15 times each week. Now it would kill me and drive me nuts, but back then it was an amazing learning curve.[8]

There were prophetic words over Matt as well, such as the time in Atlanta when Wayne Drain, a man with a developed prophetic gift, spoke over Matt and Mike, calling Mike to act as a father to Matt and indicating that the two would work together internationally. Wayne went on to say that the proof of the word he had spoken would be by way of the first two international invitations, which would be from South Africa and Australia. Soon after their return, they received two invitations to teach and lead worship. One was from Durban, South Africa. The second was from Melbourne, Australia.[9]

TIM HUGHES

Mike Pilavachi has been involved in discipling a number of younger men. Another is Tim Hughes. Mike remembers Tim as being a particularly cheeky boy at St Andrew's Chorleywood. As a youngster, Tim and a friend came up to Mike and asked if they could pray for him. Mike was delighted that such young lads had a passion to pray for others.

'OK,' said Tim, 'close your eyes and lift your hands.'

Mike did so.

Tim declared: 'In Jesus' name, we cast out the demon of ugliness!'[10]

Tim remembers being at the very first New Wine week at the age of 11 and witnessing the worship:

I'd grown up in church but I remember walking into that conference and there was this Canadian guy named Andy Park leading worship. I was stunned seeing all the people worshipping in such an intimate way. It was a revelation moment of realising these people had a relationship with God and they had such passion and devotion. I'd recently given my life to Christ, and at that conference I was filled with the Holy Spirit. Since then nothing else has seemed remotely as exciting as following God. When we got home I began to learn the guitar and just spent hours and hours learning worship songs and simply worshipping.[11]

The marked impression that particularly hit 11-year-old Tim was the idea that Jesus was present in the Spirit and in power. As Tim witnessed people falling to the floor under the power of the Holy Spirit, as he saw people healed and as he witnessed them shouting out their praises to God, it affected him deeply.[12]

Mike Pilavachi had kept an eye on Tim, and in 1996 he asked him to lead worship for the New Wine Club One age group. The following year Tim led at New Wine Youth, and then went on to lead at Soul Survivor.

Tim comments on the influences from New Wine:

The values that John Wimber held are those that churches carry now. [I learned] the values of intimacy in worship, the values of connection and being Spirit-led. We weren't just trying to sing theology; it was about a relationship and it was very much an expectation that we would encounter God. So [New Wine] very much taught me that when I'm leading worship I'm trying to facilitate space for people to engage with God. It's that two-way relationship in worship. We take a step towards God and he takes a step towards us. As we draw

near, he draws near to us. It's the sense that, as we gather,
God begins to meet with us. In worship we find healing, we
find freedom, we find conviction, we find peace and hope.

The values within New Wine have strongly affected Tim in his
leading of worship. From his observation of other conferences, he
believes there is a real value and commitment given to worship
at New Wine and Soul Survivor: 'It doesn't feel like it's just a
20-minute countdown clock, where you've got to squeeze everything in. If God's moving, we're going to go with that. It's a really
fantastic value and something that's very distinctive.'

Tim considers that the outworking of those values has particularly been seen with the renewal of the Church and with leaders
who think that the word and the Spirit don't need to be separated:

> We can actually be Bible-believing, passionate about God's
> word, but also open to his Spirit and to believing in signs
> and wonders. So I think New Wine has had a phenomenal
> impact on raising leaders throughout the UK. I believe being
> part of that Church can mean being part of a Church that is
> passionate in vision, that is risk-taking, and that is full of the
> Spirit. A Church that believes in signs and wonders.

Tim has become an internationally acclaimed worship leader and
songwriter, performing to thousands of people at large events
across the globe. His latest venture has seen him become an
ordained Church of England minister, leading Gas Street Church
in Birmingham.

BRYN HAWORTH

Andy Park wasn't the only worship leader in that first year. Bryn
Haworth led beside him, and continued to lead at New Wine for

the next four years. Bryn is an accomplished singer-songwriter and guitarist with a string of successful albums. Over the years, he has moved more into leading worship and remembers playing with Andy in the first year:

> We opened the first night's worship with 'I Believe in Jesus'.
> The songs we sang back then were simpler in structure
> than they are now – just a verse or two and a chorus. But
> lyrically they were love songs that enabled people to easily
> get engaged with the Father, Son and Holy Spirit, and for
> many of us it was the first time we were able to express our
> love for God through a song; the Holy Spirit responded to
> our praise and worship by bringing his presence into our
> midst, doing wonderful things. Precious times.[13]

LEADING AT NEW WINE

Matt Redman was also at that first New Wine gathering:

> I was at the very first conference: New Wine '89. By then
> I already had a heart to worship God through music, but I'd
> never seen anything quite like this. There we were, a few
> thousand of us packed into a huge echoey cowshed – every
> beat of the snare drum reverberating around that massive
> room for about five seconds. But it didn't matter at all – for
> through those songs something much deeper was resounding
> around the very depths of our hearts. We sang songs of
> reverence – and we sang songs of holy nearness too. There
> was so much expectation as to what God would do among
> us. Every evening we invited the Holy Spirit to increase his
> activity among us, and to increase our awareness of him. We
> were never disappointed. We were ready for his glory and we
> were ready for his grace. We were ready for his wonders too.

They say that faith is the love language of God, and perhaps that's the reason we could sense his smile over our lives in such a special way during those days.[14]

Alongside Bryn, both Matt and Tim found their feet in leading and worshipping at the New Wine gatherings, as well as at Soul Survivor. Nowadays, Matt and Tim are recognized around the world as worship leaders and both have produced a number of successful worship albums. Here's Matt again:

In 1989, during that first New Wine week, I was a 15-year-old teenager fighting some big giants in my life, but through the worship music and those moments of prayer ministry I encountered the majesty and mercy of Jesus more intensely than I ever had before. I walked away with a new hunger to seek first the kingdom of God – and with a heightened passion for worship music. That began a beautiful journey for me – just a couple of years later I was leading worship for the youth meetings there. In those gatherings we had that very same sense of newness. Each year the meetings grew, and each year more young people gave their lives to Christ. And then new songs started flowing too, as we reached for fresh ways to help a generation speak to God. Before long I was on staff and leading for the adults too – and summer after summer we experienced that same sense of sacred momentum – God at work in his marvellous, mysterious and miraculous ways.

Mike Pilavachi has some fond memories of Matt at that first New Wine week as well, especially when Andy Park prayed for Matt:

Andy Park was leading worship and one evening I remember he got down and prayed for Matt. And the Spirit came on him. Literally we had to carry Matt out of the Showering Pavilion. It was like he was drunk. I've never seen him like that ever before – or since. The look on his face! He was hot, he was sweating, he was worshipping; it was as though he was going to take off. I think there was some sort of real anointing impartation happening there.[15]

Worship from New Wine has been captured on many CDs over the years. While some recordings have been addressed to a wider audience, notably Sam Bailey's album *Gold* (2016), the heart has primarily been to serve the worship of local churches and the emphasis on songs that work well in a congregational setting. For that reason, most of the New Wine Worship CDs have been recorded live, either at summer conferences or at worship training days during the spring. The aim is to sing the songs that the Spirit is inspiring the Church to sing, while also modelling how congregations can follow the Spirit's leading in times of worship and ensure that these gathered times are not about predetermined 'set lists' but are times of encounter. New Wine's voice of worship is the voice of the Church, not of the worship leader.

Chris Sayburn took over from Sam Bailey as New Wine's Head of Worship in 2016. His concern is that songs being written and recorded genuinely serve the local church as well. After all, New Wine, argues Chris, has to be about the local church changing nations. Chris explains:

We perhaps need to think of other avenues for people who do feel called to write songs that shape culture outside of church. There is space and a real need for both. However, when we gather, I want us to be using songs that change the culture of the *Church* so the people of God are the ones shaping culture, not *songs*. This doesn't mean we can't be creative. In fact, we will need to be more creative if we are to write songs that serve the Church theologically, that are accessible musically, and that are also memorable.

As a family, we believe in the greatness and the nearness of God, in Jesus Christ, through His Spirit. As we lead musical worship I want to encourage high praise, deep intimacy and wide open spaces. Throughout our New Wine history, we as a family have been about pursuing and recognising God's presence among His people. We have to be about God's presence over and above our programmes. His glory is our purpose, His presence is our priority.[16]

New Wine's approach to worship has always been in line with that central aspect of its theology, the coming of God's kingdom in Jesus and the 'now and not yet' tension of the experience of that kingdom. The approach to worship is that it be joyful and hopeful but not triumphalist. Chris Sayburn again:

Chris Sayburn leading worship in the Main Arena

In our worship, we need to give space for the Spirit to be changing *us* if we are going to be changing nations! We must always come with expectancy and therefore give space for the Spirit to be at work in the Church and in our individual lives. Let's not limit the Spirit to the spontaneous. Can God be at work in these times? Yes! Can God's Spirit be at work when we use liturgy, light a candle, jump around, be silent, even follow a song structure? Yes! This is why those who lead worship in the family must be about leading people, not just songs or liturgy. Keep your eyes open, see what the Lord is doing and join in.

We come with expectation but we also come honestly. For some of the family when we gather there will be deep sorrow, pain and questions. This is OK, this is our story (as modelled by the honesty of the Psalms). We don't have to hide or pretend in our worship. Instead we are to come and bring the realities of life in worship to a God who is compassionate enough to care and able enough to act. It's in His presence we find comfort and perspective as well as commission.

The songs may have changed over the years, and the worship leaders certainly have. But God continues to work mightily through his Spirit. Worship brings us to his feet. It reminds us of who we are and who he is. Mary Pytches has the final words of this chapter:

I have a primary calling and that's intimacy with God. My secondary calling is what I do in ministry. But my primary calling is the relationship with God. It's being God's story, if you like. God has a purpose and plan for us and I want to be in that purpose and plan. The thing is, it's so easy to make a detour and then my story becomes the primary focus of my life. What I'm doing, even what I'm doing for God, can become the primary focus. Actually, that should never be. The primary focus is my relationship with God. If I can keep in His story, then my life, my story is the secondary thing.[17]

9   To the nations

Bruce Collins tells the international story of New Wine. It is a story of God's grace, close friendships and the moving of the Holy Spirit.

'Bruce . . . Bruce! I wonder if I could have a word with you?'

Anne Watson made her way over to me. It was the end of a long day of conference and I was tired. But always ready to listen to Anne. She has faithfully served the Lord for many years, both with her late husband, David Watson, and in more recent times as an effective leader in New Wine and the Vineyard churches.

'It's just this, Bruce. I feel the Lord is saying we need to begin to take the New Wine leaders' retreats out to other countries, rather than expect leaders to travel to attend them in the UK. I wonder whether you would please pray about that?'[1]

I did of course. And I believe it to have been a timely word from the Lord.

The early international work of New Wine had been laid down by pioneering visits to a number of countries from David and Mary Pytches, Richard and Prue Bedwell, and Barry Kissell. They attended many conferences as guest speakers. Friendships were developed in such a way that, as and when New Wine began to take off, those friendships remained and often became the stepping stone to working directly in those particular countries.

In response to Anne's word, I began to accept the invitations to visit other countries that came in as a result of leaders attending our UK events. The first was an invitation to Mike Pilavachi and myself to visit South Africa, and I still have vivid memories of our flight out. Mike was then a very nervous flyer, and as we circled before landing, things got a bit bumpy. I vividly remember how heroically he managed to hold our Boeing 747 up in the sky by his seat's armrests!

As the New Wine Network got under way in the UK, there were a number of requests for help in setting up similar networks in other countries. We were only willing to do this when it became clear that a sufficient number of significant leaders in these nations agreed together – that they wanted to start a network using New Wine's name, and that they had a clear commitment to maintaining our New Wine vision and values. They also had to accept that we would walk closely alongside them for the first five years to ensure that this was so.

After 20 years of travel, with roughly two million miles flown (and not least the impact of ageing too), my memories of the years from 1995 to 2010 prior to passing on the oversight of our international networking to Mark Aldridge have become a little blurred! But with Mark's help, what follows is a brief summary of what has been a quite remarkable story.

THE BRITISH ISLES

Work in **Ireland** started as early as 1994, not long after the Holy Spirit blessing (referred to often as the 'Toronto Blessing', reflecting its beginnings) was brought back to the UK by David Pytches,

Eleanor Mumford, and others. Literally hundreds of Irish leaders have now attended retreats. After some while, David and Hilary McClay were invited by David Pytches to lead the work in Ireland, and this led to the launch of an annual New Wine summer event from 2003 onwards which has run every year since (except 2005) and now attracts roughly 2,000 delegates to its venue at Sligo. Approximately 40 per cent come from the south, including many Catholics. A Catholic bishop is due to speak at their summer event this year so New Wine Ireland is helping to build real bridges between divided communities.

They also hold women's and men's events and an annual three-day Kingdom Intensives Conference for leaders. There are further gatherings designed to train and encourage worship leaders.

In **Wales,** the origins of New Wine Cymru also go back a long way. Barry Kissell made several visits with faith-sharing teams from St Andrew's Chorleywood in the 1980s and early 1990s. Welsh church leaders had attended the early UK conferences led by John Wimber, and came to the subsequent leaders' retreats held in Chorleywood.

In 2004 New Wine Cymru was formally established. A number of leaders' retreats and church conferences were then held, and from 2006 New Wine Cymru took over an annual summer gathering at the Royal Welsh Showground at Builth Wells, which lasted until 2009. I sensed a call to move to Wales in 2007, and soon met many church leaders, forming a completely new leadership team comprising senior leaders drawn from different church streams. Early on, it became clear that Julian Richards was called to lead us. Since then, New Wine Cymru has developed as a network focusing primarily on church leaders, and in addition the National Leaders' Conference has grown to become a popular premier event each year.

Julian exercises leadership through a National Apostolic Team, whose members lead six major regions covering Wales – each having its own regional leadership teams. This approach has paid handsome dividends. There are now over 650 church leaders in the network, all committed to New Wine's vision and values, and drawn from a wide variety of church streams – everything from Pentecostals to Catholics, as well as Fresh Expressions church plants.

Aside from regular Regional Network Days, emerging leaders' gatherings, and annual conferences specifically designed for women in leadership and equipping worship leaders, every St David's Day (1 March) a live-linked prayer meeting across the nation takes place to pray for the kingdom of God to advance in Wales.

In 2017 New Wine Cymru launched 'Mission to Wales' (an adaptation of the approach developed by The Turning in Reading), an initiative that enables church members to take the gospel out on to the streets of cities, towns and villages across Wales. In just nine days in 2017, 3,150 people prayed a prayer of commitment to the Lord, with many also being healed or strongly affected by prophetic words. Important lessons, especially in regard to follow-up, have been learned. By the end of 2018, this figure had risen to over 4,600 people.[2] It has been especially encouraging to see how this has equipped and emboldened ordinary church members to share their faith with others, not only in the mission itself but also in other circumstances of everyday life.

In **Scotland**, a summer event called the Clan Gathering was held annually at St Andrews, Fife. In addition there were several leaders' retreats and other events in venues around Scotland to help develop the network.

The Clan Gathering event grew in size over the years and had an impact on thousands of Christians across Scotland with speakers from the USA, Canada and New Wine England. The event closed after 2012, but much has been sown into Scotland.

In the **Channel Islands**, a summer New Wine event came into being on Jersey in 2005 (with 16 churches and 750 delegates) and later on in Guernsey from 2008 (with 14 churches and also up to 750 delegates). Given the small populations of these islands, these are relatively large ecumenical gatherings.

NORDIC COUNTRIES

In the Nordic countries, the work in **Finland** began early in the New Wine journey. Jorma Karanko, who had attended a leaders' retreat in Chorleywood, invited New Wine to work with him. The Finns were especially hungry and open to receive ministry in the power of the Spirit. I vividly remember speaking at a 6.30 p.m. meeting held in a beautiful Lutheran church in the centre of Helsinki. Prayer ministry started at around 7.30 p.m., but so many recipients immediately went home to urge partners and friends to come along as well to receive ministry that we only staggered out of the building around midnight!

Many visits have been made to Finland over the years by New Wine leaders to cities and retreat centres throughout the nation – from Helsinki in the south to Rovaniemi well inside the Arctic Circle! Approximately 550 Finnish church leaders (Lutheran, Free Church, and others) have attended 40 leaders' retreats and very many conferences in different cities, and there have been annual summer gatherings since 1996. Around

2,500 attended in 2018. Fresh emphasis is now being given to networking church leaders.

I have many memories of our Finnish visits. One is of a conference in Helsinki in which a group of very formally dressed Lutheran pastors watched Bishop Graham Dow delivering several people from demonic oppression. From the expressions on their faces it was obvious that these pastors had never seen (or even imagined) a bishop doing anything like that before!

In writing this I want to pay particular tribute to Simo Lintinen, who with his wife Helena gave very significant leadership in the development of New Wine Finland during its formative years. Sadly, Simo died after a short illness a few years ago. He was a very influential leader in Finland and widely respected across different church streams and in other countries too. His encouragement and friendship have meant a huge amount over the years.

Sweden is a leading country in the New Wine family of networks. David and Mary Pytches were early visitors. People who attended David's meetings were struck by unusual demonstrations of the Lord's presence and power. Subsequently, I was asked to bring teams to Andrew Thompson's church in Vargön, and he and his church became one of the early foundation stones of what developed as the new Swedish New Wine Network.

Later in 1996 I met a senior Swedish Free Church pastor called Kjell-Axel Johansson who was visiting London. Kjell-Axel invited me to bring a team to a church whose congregation he was rebuilding in central Stockholm, and this was the first of several visits there. He loved New Wine's vision and values, and soon linked Andrew Thompson and others into developing a series of leaders' retreats and church conferences. Another key connection was John Derneborg, a Pentecostal pastor, who invited me to bring a team to meetings in his church in Holmedal, Värmland.

The New Wine Sweden Network was officially launched in 1999 with Kjell-Axel Johansson as its first leader. Respected both as a church leader and Evangelical theologian, his standing among different denominations was a key factor in the way the network found wide acceptance and growth.

A regular Swedish New Wine summer conference started at Töcksfors, developing into what is now a very ecumenical gathering of around 2,000 in Vänersborg, not far from Gothenburg. In 2008 a focused 'Year of Sweden' was held when we sought to identify and develop 'storehouse churches' which would be centres of renewal; we would then network around them in a very intentional way. This was repeated in 2017.

The hundreds of New Wine events held throughout Sweden during the last 20 years have influenced Swedish Christianity well beyond the New Wine Sweden Network itself. For example, some of the largest Christian conferences and gatherings in Sweden have been addressed – and had their ministry teams trained – by New Wine leaders from Sweden and the UK.

While there are no formal New Wine networks in **Norway, Denmark** and **Estonia**, New Wine leaders have been invited to serve very many churches there over the last 25 years, and relationships continue to develop.

EUROPE

Dutch Reformed pastors Dick and Jeanette Westerkamp visited St Andrew's Chorleywood from 1992 onwards, attending leaders' retreats, and they then invited David and Mary Pytches to their church in Houten, the **Netherlands**. New Wine leaders' retreats were started in Houten in 2000 and ran annually until 2016. Retreats to develop leaders in their leadership skills and refresh them in their kingdom DNA are now offered. Summer gatherings started in 2004 and have grown annually, with over 6,000 delegates in 2017.

We encountered some fairly robust theological challenges from pastors with Reformed backgrounds. I remember one retreat at which a well-known and able theologian and pastor was asking challenging questions during teaching sessions and in coffee and meal breaks over the first three days. On the fourth day, the Lord spoke directly to him through a very accurate prophetic ministry from Freda Meadows (a member of my Harrow-based team) and he was then so overwhelmed by the Holy Spirit that he was unable to move or speak for a few hours! Soon afterwards he became a leading figure in New Wine Netherlands and has been really helpful in dealing with some of the public challenges thrown at its work in the media by pastors of other persuasions.

In **France, Russia** and **Czechia**, we have seen multiple visits by leaders from the UK, and strong partnerships with churches in **Germany** and the Umbria region of **Italy** are beginning to grow.

SOUTH AFRICA

From a first visit in 1995, members of the New Wine team have regularly visited South Africa, making a significant investment there. Led by Nigel Juckes, a widely respected leader of St Agnes' Church near Durban, networks developed in Kwa-Zulu Natal and around Port Elizabeth, in Cape Town and in the Northern Province. Many leaders' retreats and church-based conferences have been held. Nigel Juckes commented:

As the first leader of New Wine in South Africa, I'm extremely grateful for the kingdom perspective on ministry that New Wine brought. It changed our focus from a preoccupation with church activities to seeking to see God's kingdom come in power. Spirit-led worship and the release of gifting and leadership through prophetic prayer have been significant. The word 'You only get to keep what you give away' became a watchword for us. And we have so appreciated the international connection.

NORTH AMERICA

In **Canada**, I had the privilege of attending the first New Wine summer gathering held at a campsite out on the prairies of Alberta. Since then, there has been a mix of retreats and regional conferences around the summer gathering, which moved to Strathmore. Work also developed in British Columbia, serving churches in Vancouver and Abbotsford, and it amazed us to see how many people from these churches were willing to travel over 700 miles through the Rockies to the summer gathering!

Although the New Wine movement has formally ended in Canada, many of those who were influenced are now leading lights in the new Anglican Church in North America.

Following a visit to a Shepton Mallet summer gathering, an Episcopalian leader called Steve Wood invited several of us to visit his church in Mount Pleasant, South Carolina. As a result, a New Wine **USA** summer event was started in June 2005 and ran for several years. This too has now stopped, with the Anglican Church in North America movement having taken over a majority of church leaders' time and energy in place of New Wine.

NEW ZEALAND

Following early visits from Barry Kissell and David Pytches, New Wine New Zealand was formed through a visit by John Coles and myself in 2003. Since 2005 the summer gatherings have grown to attract over 2,000 people, and the database shows that since 2005 over 10,000 people have come to events from 800 different churches. This number represents around 40 per cent of all the churches in New Zealand!

New Wine New Zealand has now come to be a trusted, respected church movement. This has allowed its leaders to develop some interesting initiatives. For example, they have recently used their networks to put the Bible Society's Action Bible into the libraries of 2,000 primary and 800 secondary schools, as well as providing copies for every prison in New Zealand.

Mark Melluish teaching at New Wine New Zealand 2010

OTHER PARTNERSHIPS

New Wine **India** is developing rapidly. There are now over 1,000 churches in the network. After a visit to India in 2014, John Coles commented that 'this is the nearest thing to the New Testament I have ever known'. This continues to be the case. A visit by a team from New Wine England in November 2018 was marked by significant healing miracles, with the added encouragement that the team's role on this occasion was much more about coaching local church leaders who were giving the input to their fellow pastors.

Exciting New Wine partnerships are growing with churches in **Brazil**, the **United Arab Emirates** and **Pakistan** – some of

John Coles, Gary Weston and team with the New Wine India team

which may soon develop into fully fledged New Wine country networks.

A VISIBLE KINGDOM

As I look back on the international work, one clear manifestation is a visible work of the Holy Spirit. Paul says that the 'manifestation of the Spirit is given for the common good'.[3] This has been of primary importance in the development of all our networks, especially seeing the Holy Spirit fall visibly on people in times of ministry after talks, and prophetic ministry being exercised also.

The role of especially gifted prophetic ministers such as Freda Meadows and Loraine Craig in the work I was doing to help develop new networks truly did 'prepare the way of the Lord'.[4] I have several times seen rather wary church elders soften and open up rapidly to receive all we brought through prophetic ministry to them prior to a church conference. The Lord sent his first leaders out in pairs, and it has been a huge personal blessing to travel with teams. Rather than being all about one person's gifts, this models a wholesome complementarity of ministry as a team to leaders and their churches.

We aim to integrate a thoroughly biblical understanding of Jesus' 'kingdom gospel' and ministry together with a wise 'naturally supernatural' set of values in how that ministry is expressed. Unlike many international ministries that hold conferences in other countries, New Wine offers ongoing, committed partnership and real friendship. Those friendships have been a key to our success internationally, and will continue to be so as Mark Aldridge takes on this work.

Group photo from International Forum 2014

MISSIONAL MOVEMENTS

The Lord equipped his first leaders through the offer of relationship while exercising and modelling the ministry of the kingdom, and New Wine has walked a long walk with countries even when progress in those countries has sometimes been slow.

Here, I believe, is a prophetic pointer for our future development. We read in Acts that the Holy Spirit said: 'Set apart for me Barnabas and Saul for the work to which I have called them.'[5] And in Ephesians, Paul teaches us that the Church is 'built on the foundation of the apostles and prophets, with Christ Jesus himself as the chief cornerstone'.[6]

Leaders who lead large churches may be apostolically gifted, by which we mean that they are able to initiate kingdom activity across a wider region or nation, but the demands of leading larger churches usually make it either very difficult or, in a lot of cases, excessively taxing to fulfil a wider apostolic role. My experience in Wales has shown very clearly how 'setting apart' a leader with apostolic gifting can be very effective in rapidly developing networks of significant church leaders, especially when directly supported by a 'Barnabas'-type prophetic teaching ministry. This not only brings renewal to individual Christians and churches, but also enables networks to evolve into truly missional movements. I therefore believe that we need to further develop our understanding, practice and encouragement of apostolic ministries at home and abroad.

John Wimber once said to David Pytches: 'If God has blessed you and your church through this visit, decide to give away to others everything he has given you.'[7] This we have tried to do as we develop friendships and networks around the world.

10 Church planting

John Coles records the ways in which New Wine has partnered with the planting of new churches in the UK.

When David Pytches came back to England, he found the Church of England to be more hidebound by rules and regulations than the Anglican Church in which he had been a bishop in Chile. His experience there had been stretched by what he had studied and what he had seen. In his reading of Roland Allen's two seminal books, *Missionary Methods: St. Paul's or ours*[1] and *The Spontaneous Expansion of the Church and the Causes that Hinder It*, he had recognized the need for releasing not only the leadership but also the ministry of the Church to indigenous people:

> This then is what I mean by spontaneous expansion. I mean the expansion which follows the unexhorted and unorganized activity of individual members of the Church explaining to others the Gospel which they have found for themselves; I mean the expansion which follows the irresistible attraction of the Christian Church for men who see its ordered life, and are drawn to it by desire to discover the secret of a life which they instinctively desire to share; I mean also the expansion of the Church by the addition of new Churches.[2]

David had also seen this in the rapid multiplication of Pentecostal churches in Chile through the leadership of empowered lay people. And he unexpectedly discovered that his churches in Chile had become grandparents – the churches he had planted had now planted other churches without his involvement! When he left he had successfully argued for the appointment of a Chilean bishop to continue this, freed from the control of the UK.

DECLINE

On David's arrival back in England in 1977, he discovered that almost no one in the Church of England was talking about church planting as either a current reality or a necessity. He was alarmed at the rapid decline in churchgoing in England since he had left for Chile 17 years earlier. Although a significant house-church movement had begun in the 1970s, leading to the planting of many new neo-Pentecostal churches – grouped together in Ichthus under Roger Forster's leadership, in Pioneer under Gerald Coates, and in Newfrontiers under Terry Virgo – the Church of England had not yet woken up to this aspect of what God was doing worldwide. Peter Wagner brought this into full view in 1990 in his book *Church Planting for a Greater Harvest*, which included these now famous words: 'The single most effective evangelistic methodology under heaven is planting new churches.'[3]

Bob Hopkins was one of the first Anglicans to write about church planting in his 1988 Grove booklet, *Church Planting: Models for mission in the Church of England*.[4] Bob caricatured parish boundaries as 'a line drawn round thousands of people to protect them from hearing the gospel'.[5] David Pytches, in his frustration at the slow pace at which the Church of England was embracing church planting, later dramatically referred to parish boundaries as 'the condom of the Anglican Church, impeding natural reproduction'.[6]

JOINED AT THE HIP

From the very first New Wine event in 1989 until 2000, Bob Hopkins held seminars on church planting for anyone who was interested in learning more and putting it into practice. In that time over 1,000 leaders (including the current Archbishop of Canterbury, Justin Welby) were individually encouraged at Bob's seminars, which included an invitation to a one-to-one consultation with Bob and his wife Mary regarding the application of the principles he taught. Bob had sensed God calling him to church planting in the Anglican Church in the late 1970s. Living in Chorleywood, and a member of Christ Church, he went to the meeting for church leaders hosted in 1981 by David Pytches at which John Wimber spoke about church planting. Bob and Mary were deeply influenced by the Spirit. They gathered friends and started praying with others about what they should do. Some of those whom Bob consulted weren't very encouraging of his vision. In contrast Gerald Coates, leader of the Pioneer group of churches, said: 'Go and make it happen.'

In 1983 Bob and Mary went on a faith-sharing trip with Barry Kissell. After a time of prayer and fasting, Barry suggested that Bob and Mary should take a team to St Helens; the challenge was to help plant a church in the tenth most deprived parish in the Liverpool diocese! It was another year before a team willing to face that challenge moved together to Liverpool, but the anointing from the Spirit for teaching and leading in church planting fell on Bob at almost the same time as the anointing for leading an empowering movement of the Spirit in the UK fell on

David Pytches. New Wine and church planting were joined at the hip from then on.

CHURCH-PLANTING CONFERENCE

By 1987 a number of those affected by the move of the Spirit in the UK (which John Wimber had encouraged) hosted a National Church Planting Conference at Holy Trinity Brompton. The church there had just sent out its first church-planting team. About 200 people gathered to learn together at this first conference, rising to 700 by 1991.

I was one of the delegates at the first conference, having listened to John Wimber's teaching series 'Church planting: planning your history in advance',[7] and realizing that in reality I was planting a new church alongside the old at St Barnabas Woodside Park, London. The obvious question was: can I really do this in the Church of England? At that conference I found others who had answered the same question so positively that I felt the Lord reaffirm my call to the Anglican Church.

Most of that time, I worked at trying to lead a contemporary Anglican church accessible to present-day culture. Initially that was in a traditional Anglican building, but since leaving St Barnabas in 2011, Anne and I have been co-leading 'The Space', a home church in north London. This has drawn unchurched and de-churched people from a wide geographic area, leading them to faith in Jesus and seeing them integrated into churches closer to where they live.

VINEYARD CHURCHES

David Watson, one of the early leaders of renewal in the UK who had encouraged David Pytches to invite John Wimber to visit the country in the early 1980s, had encouraged John not to plant in England. However, when John and Eleanor Mumford were so deeply affected by the Spirit, John Wimber recognized this as God's call on their lives. By 2018 there were 120 Vineyard churches in the UK and Ireland, all seeking to reach the previously unreached. John and Eleanor have been significant speakers at many New Wine events, and were remarkably used by God to usher into England another wave of the power of the Spirit in 1994, known as the Toronto Blessing. John and Debby Wright, their successors as leaders of the Vineyard UK, led Venue 2 at Shepton Mallet for many years and remain invited speakers at our conferences. We thank God for the birth of the Vineyard movement in this country, and the contribution it has made towards the re-evangelization of our nation.

Following the early church-planting conferences, David Pytches began to plant a variety of churches around the Chorleywood area:

> With St Andrew's so full we felt like a pregnant woman wanting to give birth. Regular members were complaining that they had to arrive half an hour early to obtain a seat in the main building of their own church![8]

St Andrew's planted twice within their parish, but because many people had come from outside, David now came up against the impenetrable parish boundary problem. It was at this point that he caused controversy through his comment that parish boundaries acted like a contraceptive, blocking new life. While the leaders of Holy Trinity Brompton were successful in working with their bishop to gain permission to cross parish boundaries, the same favour was not extended to David. However, some lay people were sufficiently trained in leadership that on moving from Chorleywood they planted churches in their new locations. Some of these became Vineyard churches.

SOUL SURVIVOR WATFORD

Life begets life, and healthy churches naturally reproduce. In 1993 Mike Pilavachi, David Pytches' youth worker, had a vision for working with young people from all over Watford. 'Dreggs Café' was launched by a team of 12 who initially met to pray in a front room on a Wednesday evening and dream together about how they might provide an atmosphere where young people could be appropriately cared for and loved, and which would spark an interest in Jesus.

A few months later they started a monthly evening service on Sundays in a school, and it quickly became a church for young people. Numbers of slightly older people who had been commuting to Chorleywood to church realized that a new church had now started in Watford, and Soul Survivor Watford grew quickly in numbers, visibility and notoriety. To those concerned, in the diocesan hierarchy and among other church leaders, David and Mike's defence was that it was 'an experiment' to reach unreached teenagers, in a way that no other church in Watford was doing at that time. But a pattern was now set for entrepreneurial apostolic leaders to start things which others, more pastorally minded, would later find they had to accommodate. Mike Pilavachi is now an ordained Anglican, Soul Survivor Watford is a recognized Anglican church, and hundreds have been added to the kingdom as a result of its conception!

NEW GROUND

In 1991 Charlie Cleverly, an ordained Anglican at that time working in Cranham Park, Essex, and who later became an influential leader in New Wine circles, wrote about the need for the Church of England to adopt this strategy for the re-evangelization of the UK in his prophetically entitled book *Church Planting: Our future hope*.[9] David Pytches addressed the need for new structures to enable evangelism and church in his book *New Wineskins*,[10] published in 1991.

All this activity provoked an official response. In 1994 the Church of England published a report entitled *Breaking New Ground*.[11] By 2003 Archbishop Rowan Williams was speaking about a 'mixed economy' of church to meet these new challenges. This was amplified by the 2004 report, *Mission-Shaped Church*, which sought to reflect what was already happening and then to make recommendations for the future practice of this pioneering mission.

One of the most difficult things the Church of England has had to embrace is its willingness to let go of some of its central control in order to let 'apostolic leaders' try new ways of reaching the unreached. Its first loosening of control came through the creation of Bishops' Mission Orders in 2008, which enabled the authorizing of 'Fresh Expressions' of church after appropriate collaboration across parish boundaries. The *Mission-Shaped Church* report called for the identification, selection and training of pioneers:

> Priority and attention needs to be given . . . to the identification and training of leaders for pioneering missionary projects. The possibility of a call to such work needs to

be specifically identified in the vocational process. It is then important that they are not pressed into becoming ministers of existing churches but are deployed in pioneering contexts.[12]

New Wine has sought to be a network which has encouraged such pioneering apostolic leadership, among its lay delegates as well as its ordained church leaders. Jon Soper is one such pioneering apostolic leader. Jon and his wife Jo felt called to plant a church in Exeter in 2005. At the time, there was not a warm welcome. Nonetheless they went ahead, and as the church grew through evangelism and compassionate ministry among unreached people, the Anglican authorities began to recognize the validity of the Sopers' call and the authenticity of their congregation as an Anglican church. In 2009 the church became recognized and authorized as Exeter Network Church and as one of the first official Bishop's Mission Orders in the Church of England. It is now celebrated as one of the outstanding healthy and growing churches in the Exeter diocese.

MORE GROWTH

The Sopers moved to Exeter from a curacy at St Mary's Bryanston Square in London, where John Peters had planted a church in 2000. John has been a regular speaker at New Wine summer conferences, and radical church-planting is in his blood. He has now developed a network of churches, working with ex-members and former staff. This includes four churches in the USA, one in New Zealand, one in Germany and a further couple in the UK. One of these, KXC (King's Cross Church), is led by Pete Hughes, the son of one of the first Bible teachers at New Wine, John

Hughes. Started in 2010, it has now outgrown its hired premises and is seeking a larger, more permanent place to meet. It has a great vision:

> We want to be a church that recklessly gives itself away to God, each other and the people of King's Cross and beyond. As a hub of creativity, courage and compassion, we want to bring people together to build a community where all can flourish, giving the best of our time, energy, and creativity to see God's kingdom transform the spiritual, social, and physical landscape of King's Cross.[13]

When Henry Kendal took over from me as Vicar of St Barnabas in 2006, he continued to lead the church in responding to planting opportunities. In 2007 Helen Shannon moved on to an urban estate, wonderfully named Strawberry Vale, and began 'church@ five', leading initially as a lay believer, and subsequently being ordained in 2010. She now oversees another church plant on a nearby estate, and is a leading architect in Bishop Ric Thorpe's National Estate Churches Network, and a contributor to the Archbishops' Estates Evangelism Task Force, chaired by the Bishop of Burnley, Philip North. Philip says, 'The vision is a thriving, loving Christian church on every single large estate. That's not a building – we're talking about church as community of people.'[14]

Other New Wine churches have a similar commitment to urban mission. Mark Melluish at St Paul's Ealing, in partnership with Eden,[15] commissioned Mark Tate to lead the Grove Missional Community with a team of eight on to the Gurnell Grove Estate. Pulled together by a mutual love for sharing Jesus and a heart for otherwise unreached places in London, particularly estates, the team took part in the church-planting course at the Centre for

Church Planting and Growth,[16] while remaining a part of the wider church family of St Paul's. Their desire was not just to be an external entity sent in to bless the community, but to become a part of the community itself and bless it from the inside. They began to move on to the estate in 2016, prayer walking during the week, and trying to gather a community of non-believers, leading them towards a relationship with Jesus rather than attracting Christians already living in the area. Their integration into the estate, modelled by Mark in his election as Chair of the Residents' Association, has resulted in the community growing through a full range of activities from gardening to worship, and from kids' activities to bingo, all undergirded by prayer walking and love.

URBAN PLANTING

One of the more unusual church-planting exercises is the 'Saturday Gathering' in Halifax. Linda Maslen was a leader in the team that set up a food bank in Halifax. This naturally grew to become a drop-in centre too. As Linda explains:

> The aspiration was not only to give out food but also to build relationships that would draw people to Jesus. After a year of running as a food bank, we felt that God was asking us to introduce Him into the Drop In more dynamically, so we set up a prayer ministry team and we were surprised at just how many people, when given the opportunity, wanted us to pray with them. Then, as we prayed, God answered and we saw people wanting to come to know Him better.[17]

The problem was that those reached through the drop-in centre were not integrating well into the church in Halifax. Linda had to make a difficult decision:

The people we were trying to involve did not know how to behave in the church setting; they did not know when to be quiet – or not; some could not read the service sheet or the newsletter; they asked questions we didn't really want them to ask! They also couldn't hide what they were feeling, expressing their emotions in ways that far too many of us would consider inappropriate in 'normal church' – a place where the wearing of a 'mask' to hide emotions is very much expected by the majority of people for most of the time. Before long, it was a struggle for both the new Christians and the congregation to cope as it really served to expose those weaknesses.[18]

As a result, the 'Saturday Gathering' started as a pilot in 2012. It was an immediate success. The new Christians grew in their faith, and it wasn't long before they were asking to be baptized. On 11 January 2014, 19 men, women and children were baptized and confirmed. The baptism was by full immersion in a portable baptism tank. As the service progressed, another six came forward and wanted to be baptized on the day. For the visiting bishop, it was the most 'messy' service he had presided at, but he enjoyed every minute. Over 80 people came along to watch and participate, some from the local churches, but many were friends and family of those being baptized – most of whom had never been in a church before.

As Linda explains, through initiatives such as the Saturday Gathering they are 'infiltrating other communities as influencers'. There are now two Saturday Gathering congregations and a 'Thursday Gathering'. A third Saturday Gathering is in the planning stages. Linda explains that even more is planned:

We like to go to a hill top overlooking the town, and there we get a sense of the dark places where God is calling us to

Halifax baptism

be present and pray. We noticed a café at the town centre bus station and we are hoping soon to start a community hub there, working with other church leaders who see the opportunity for mission. So for us the dreams are just getting bigger. We are so privileged to be able to join in all that God is doing in Calderdale. We know this new wave of God is just at its beginning so we are excited to see what else is next for us.[19]

UNITED OFFERING

In 2016 New Wine gave part of its 'United' offering to enable the second Saturday Gathering to start in another part of Halifax, and since then the Thursday Gathering has also been launched.

Significant partnerships have grown with the town council and other civic authorities, including the provision of accommodation and a meeting place. The partnership between a church so committed to evangelism and the council is possible because of the obvious transformation in the lives of so many who appeared beyond the statutory provision of the council, and because the Cinnamon Trust[20] has independently assessed that the church's ministries would cost the council around £6 million per year if it had to deliver them. This is undergirded by Linda's understanding that God himself is engaged in mission, both within and beyond the boundaries of church.

Similarly, in 2013 Ian Parkinson, the vicar of All Saints' Marple, commissioned his curate, Gareth Robinson, to plant a church on an impoverished estate in Offerton. Gareth was well versed in approaches to discipling young adults, developing missional communities and training leaders. He moved into Offerton with his wife Lizzy and their three children. The church was named Glo (God Loves Offerton): 'The vision was to bring faith, hope and love to Offerton: faith in God's love shown through Jesus, hope for those who are lost and lonely, and love for the broken and busted.'[21]

Meeting for worship each Sunday afternoon at Offerton Community Centre, running Kids Café, Glo Youth, Playtime toddler groups, opening a shop, and a number of other projects in partnership, the church has seen many come to faith in Jesus who were previously completely outside the influence of any church. This includes a large number of disaffected teenagers and young adults – the 'missing generations' in most churches.

While leading Glo, Gareth began to develop a training course and website for would-be church planters, 'The Bridge', which is 'raising the profile of mission, multiplication and church planting across New Wine'.[22]

Gareth's commitment to church planting and his diplomacy in working with sometimes hesitant bishops has been one of the more significant factors in changing the climate for church planting in the Church of England. Gareth is now leading a new plant into Salford, using the model of revitalizing an almost redundant church with a well-trained leader and a team that includes a worship leader, a kids' leader and an administrator. This model has proved highly successful, both in city centres and in the more middle-class areas of our cities. And the support of church planters and celebration of their 'success' in their network is really empowering.

INCARNATIONAL

New Wine has always sought to encourage a wide variety of approaches to church planting, including an incarnational approach. A working definition of incarnational church might be 'the immersion of one's self into a local culture and "becoming Jesus" to that culture'. A sensitive incarnation in a community can precede the discovery of the best way forward in mission. This is the approach developed by Fresh Expressions in their empowering *Mission-Shaped Ministry Course*.[23]

One such initiative is led by Paul Bradbury and his wife Emily in Poole, Dorset:

> Reconnect is a Christian community focussed on connecting with people with little or no Christian background. Our life together is based on small groups meeting in people's homes at various times in the week. Our mission is based on our commitment to living out the gospel in our daily

lives and to using our natural gifts and interests to connect with others. We have a pattern of community gatherings on Sundays which includes community action, a shared meal and community worship. Members of Reconnect have started a number of other small communities based around film, creativity, walking, hospitality and beer making! In all these ways we serve people, build relationships together and offer ways in which people can begin to explore the Christian faith.[24]

Paul has recently taken a lead in informally networking with others in New Wine who are involved in such 'out-of-the-box' ventures that are not supported by a local sending church.

Some church planting can be short term – we should not always expect a long-term church community with a building! On the website of the Anglican Church Planting Initiative, started by Bob Hopkins, a story is told of Captain Steve Hunt and his wife Emma who pioneered a plant on a needy council estate in the parish of Cove, Farnborough. The plant initially thrived but closed sooner than was hoped:

This story should not be simply seen as one of failure. During the significant number of years that this pioneer initiative lasted, a remarkable number of those discipled in the heat of this demanding mission field responded to callings to recognised leadership in the national church and to overseas mission.[25]

PRINCIPLES

New Wine isn't a denomination or a brand, but works with local churches to see the kingdom extended. As it has sometimes been expressed: 'New Wine doesn't plant churches but New Wine churches plant churches.' This is significant in the subsequent oversight of those churches – it rests on the shoulders of the mother church, not New Wine. That's why it's not really possible to tell how many churches have been planted 'in association with New Wine'. This doesn't mean that there is no strategy to support church planting, though. It's clear that many leaders have been emboldened and empowered through their belonging to a Network with growing knowledge and experience about church planting, and one that supports them in taking such initiatives. Regular training days, mentoring groups and leadership retreats help to give the community the support that pioneers and planters so often lack. Since 2016 part of the New Wine offering at United has been given to enable Network churches to plant new initiatives. From 2019 the church-planting strategy has developed to include work with the leaders of larger churches, of all denominations, enabling and encouraging them to take more responsibility in planting churches that will in turn plant more churches.

Initially, some operated on the premise of 'it's easier to obtain forgiveness than permission'. But that has changed. Even by the time another closing Brethren Assembly Hall was offered to St Barnabas Woodside Park, in 2001, the church-planting climate had changed significantly. The local Anglican vicar, despite being of a more liberal churchmanship himself, welcomed the idea and offer of a new initiative that would aim 'to reach people we aren't reaching', and so a team of 18 went under the leadership of Mike Pavlou. Despite various ups and downs of church life (common to all churches), the plant is thriving, now at capacity, and is about to move into a local primary school for its Sunday meetings.

THIRTY YEARS ON

Thirty years on from the first church-planting seminars at New Wine, the climate for church planting in the Church of England is very positive. As part of a national strategy, finances are being released to develop 'Resource Churches' which will foster future church-plant leaders, giving additional training and experience to the next generation of planters in places that have experienced growth. This is part of the overall 'Renewal and Reform' programme within the Church of England.

A significant number of churches in the New Wine Network are becoming designated Resource Churches in their diocese.

John McGinley, the vicar of Holy Trinity Leicester, has overseen significant numerical growth and is now a leader in church planting in the diocese. The church is officially one of the newly recognized Resource Churches in the Church of England – given extra resources to train, develop and deploy church planters. Leaders who have been recognized in a similar way include Paul Harcourt (All Saints' Woodford Wells, Diocese of Chelmsford) and Martyn Taylor (St George's Stamford, Diocese of Lincoln).

Martyn has been the rector of St George's Stamford since 2003, and was first involved as a curate from 1996. St George's has grown as a market town Resource Church, first by filling up all the available space in the building at St George's over three Sunday services, and then by multiplying smaller spin-off congregations within the parish. This eventually led to Martyn being licensed to the neighbouring diocese of Peterborough, as St George's is literally on the border. Turnaround Teams, small groups of lay leaders who can help revitalize the local church, have been sent into nearby Peterborough villages, and this has led to further growth and influence. In 2017 St George's recruited a Bishop's

Mission Order post with a brief to establish midweek discipleship groups across three deaneries in south Lincolnshire.

John McGinley became Vicar of Holy Trinity Leicester in 2009, having worked in the Leicester diocese in Hinckley for nine years where he saw many added to the church. He inherited Holy Trinity as a church with a Charismatic tradition but which was no longer on the cutting edge of mission. John re-engineered it around 'missional communities', empowering more lay people in leadership and giving them responsibility for evangelism and mission. The church has grown numerically. The original building was remodelled in 2018, with the church now hiring the 900-seater Haymarket Theatre on a monthly basis as the missional communities celebrate together.

John has since become Priest in Charge of the nearby Emmaus parish with its two church centres, and of the Holy Apostles parish with its two church centres. They have also planted a non-geographic church, Imprint, and have overseen the appointments of leaders to these churches. Imprint Church, led by Wole Agbaje, who is in his early twenties, is a wonderful example of a contemporary multi-ethnic church and has grown rapidly. A network of revitalized churches is developing around Leicester with similar vision and values to those of Holy Trinity. John has also pioneered a diocesan-funded discipleship training programme for the diocese, based on the New Wine Discipleship Year, preparing young people for future leadership in the wider Church. His latest book helps explains missional practice in more detail.[26]

Three principles undergird all of this commitment to church planting. The first is: 'If God blesses you, give it away.' This is what John Wimber said to David Pytches on his first visit to

St Andrew's in 1981. The second is: 'Faith is spelt R.I.S.K.' – another John Wimber saying. All these ventures have involved some risk; no one can predict fruitfulness in advance, and each team has had to faithfully seek God for guidance, for strategy, for resources, and for courage to continue through difficult times. The third principle is that one person may plant, another person may water, 'but God gives the increase'.[27] This means that we work together with others, and we can't and won't take credit for what God himself has done. To God be the glory.

11 Our Place and accessible church

Heather Holgate and Naomi Graham tell the amazing story of providing an unconditional welcome for everyone at the New Wine gathering, irrespective of the challenge.

The New Wine summer gathering – what a wonderful family week! Time with friends old and new. Music and worship alongside life-changing teaching. Fun and laughter! Activities for all; space to relax, to be refreshed and spiritually recharged. Does that sound too good to be true? Is that really everybody's experience?

WHAT IF . . . ?

What if your child dislikes being in crowds so much so that he hits out at others or runs away? What if your daughter cannot walk and uses a wheelchair to get around; she gets stuck in the mud, soaked with rain, and cannot go on the bouncy castle with her friends? What if your son eats the sugar from bowls in other people's tents – because there are no doors to close? What if he soils his clothes and bedding and there is a queue for the washrooms that is far too long to tolerate? What if other people look at you and you feel their criticism for 'not controlling your child's behaviour'? What if you feel left out because your family cannot do the things that other families do? That is the question that was put to a number of families at the summer conference in 2003: 'What if . . .?'

In response to some signs stuck on lamp posts, a small group of about 12 people met over coffee and doughnuts (yes, those yummy fresh doughnuts from the food court!) to try and answer the question, 'What would it take to make the New Wine summer gathering a better experience for your family; what if . . .?' As that group sat and dreamed together, Heather Holgate remembers being struck by the practical things that people identified (for example, a washing machine) and also by how much pain people had experienced at the hands of the church 'family':

> There are certain things about a showground in Somerset that one cannot change – that long drive down the A303 and the weather, but we had made a start – we had asked people what they needed and we had listened. So in 2004, with the blessing of the New Wine leadership, 'Our Place' was born.[1]

LAUGHTER AND TEARS

Our Place was to be a place where people could do life together, where they could learn how to love one another, to love themselves and to experience God's love more fully. *Our* Place was to be a safe space, where people could be themselves, where bedding was washed, paints spilt, muddy feet cleaned, mistakes made, laughter shared and tears dried. *Our* Place was to be a place where it was recognized and fully accepted that life was messy for everyone! In many ways this was counter-cultural at a time when making things look good and doing things well was upheld as the gold standard – a standard that many people felt they could never achieve.

Initially, Our Place included four streams of activities: one for children who found it too challenging to be in the large venues; a second for those who wanted support in the large groups catering for children, teens and young adults; a third for teenagers looking to develop a peer group and see God's love at work in their own lives; and one for parents who were exhausted and often felt alone, but who had so much to give.

ROOF BREAKING

At the time when Our Place was beginning to take shape, a number of the team had been struck by the events related in Luke 5.18-20 where four men, acting as advocates for their paralysed friend, broke through the roof of a house to bring him into the presence of Jesus. The team felt called to break through roofs – not always an easy job and not always acceptable! Heather explains:

> When we looked at the ministry of Jesus, we saw someone who included people and did not turn them away. The concepts of working together, inclusion, and never ever turning people away became part of the foundation of Our Place.

The principle of never turning people away was learned early on. Heather remembers standing in Our Place, probably sheltering from the rain, feeling totally out of her depth and yet incredibly sure of herself and of her God:

> I had just met a young girl and her family during regis-
> tration who wanted to attend her age-group activities. In

order to do so, she required the support of someone who could communicate using British Sign Language (BSL). I had responded positively to their request for help, saying, 'That's not a problem at all . . . go and pitch your tent and come back in a couple of hours and I'll introduce you to your helper.'

Knowing we did not have anybody on team who was able to sign proficiently in BSL, I gathered a few team members together and as we stood there we prayed, telling God of this young girl's need, of our lack of skills and our strong desire to see his kingdom value of welcome lived out at New Wine and in his Church. As we opened our eyes, we saw someone come in through the door. She came up to us and said, 'I'm a proficient BSL signer. Is there anything I can do to help you?' Talk about timing! Knowing without a shadow of a doubt that our God is a generous God who welcomes us all and provides all we need, we never ever turned anyone away from Our Place after that.

The physical venue that was Our Place included a washing machine and tumble drier that washed and spun so regularly that the floor shuddered beneath their feet and they soon learned not to use them during times of quiet reflection and prayer! The ministry of 'laundry' proved to be one of the most valuable and servant-hearted ministries at a New Wine gathering.

HOSPITALITY

The kitchenette produced tea and coffee – added to which were delicious cakes contributed by team members. The offering of a welcome meant that practical hospitality was almost continual. The volunteers believed their biggest and best skill was an ability to smile, no matter what. For parents and carers there were comfortable sofas to sit on (thanks to Freecycle) and quiet spaces to pray and sleep. For the young adults there was a videogame console, games to play, crafts to enjoy and beanbags to lounge in. The children's area was bright with soft play equipment, a ball pool, a prayer throne and lots of messy shaving foam. What had started out as a box of toys and wet-wipes in the first years of New Wine gatherings now fills numerous garages and lofts around the country! In Shepton Mallet, the numbers in Our Place grew to include on average 100 families and 70 team members each week. As the week expanded, so too did the Our Place venue, growing from one wooden building with a leaking roof, to two marquees together with a wooden building with a patched roof – and many buckets! Heather remembers one of the earlier times of welcoming people:

> We learned the importance of 'unconditional welcome' one summer when John Coles came to visit Our Place, bringing with him a man from his church who was homeless at the time. The children were in a circle on the floor singing together. Without prompting, a little girl of four who found it difficult to express herself with words stood up, went to the two men and, taking each of them by the hand, said 'Come', pulling them into the circle to worship with us. Millie showed us how to welcome people with what she could do, regardless of who they were, their abilities, knowledge or position in society.

As well as singing, worship included drumming with buckets, jumping with Maasai warriors, swinging in a hammock, rolling on the floor, singing with worship leader Brian Doerksen – himself a father of children with additional needs – and bouncing on trampolines. Prayers were expressed with bubbles, tearing of paper, splashing in water, walking or being pushed around labyrinths, and just being still. The image of 20 or more children lying on the floor, soaking in God's presence while under a parachute, is one that astounded the team, time and time again. It was surely not natural for children with so many varying abilities to be together and to be so quiet at the same time; surely the Holy Spirit was at work. Finding inclusive and accessible ways to teach, learn, pray, worship and play required a creativity that in itself became an expression of the nature of God the Creator.

LEARNING

Alongside the visible venue and activities of Our Place, there has always been a strong emphasis on learning from one another. There

Volunteers working with children and young adults with additional needs in Our Place, 2017

has always been a mix of people on the team: people who have parented children with additional needs, professionals who bring with them a vast array of knowledge, and people who themselves have additional needs, both seen and unseen. As a team there has been a heavy investment in this area, utilizing every opportunity to better love and serve one another.

One such example is learning the skills needed to communicate with others. Some people have difficulty expressing themselves with words; others cannot physically articulate what they know they want to say. And some cannot hear words spoken, with others not understanding their meaning. During team times, there would be an exploration of fun activities and different ways to communicate with one another: sign language, facial expressions, written symbols, objects of reference, movement, gestures, vocalizations, and most importantly, listening with not just ears but eyes and bodies too. Heather explains:

> As we learned new skills and put them into practice, so we learned how better to communicate with God, allowing the Holy Spirit to groan within us (Romans 8.26), *hearing* God's hand in the tangible world around us, and learning to truly listen. Our God is not limited in his communication with us; he longs to communicate with us and he is surely a God far beyond words.

Living in a world that was far from perfect, many wrestled with the concept of physical healing. What did healing mean for someone who was created in God's image and yet the people of this earth wanted them to be different – to be 'healed'? Having said that, the team did pray and did experience miraculous answers to prayers; but still they wrestled.

Part of this wrestling extended to the sessions held for siblings of those who had additional needs. Year after year the team saw young people come back to Our Place to be together, to cry, to rage, laugh and pray, allowing God to minister into their messy world.

SHARING WITH THE WIDER CHURCH

As the team learned together in Our Place, they became increasingly aware that for 51 weeks of the year many families had very different experiences of the church family from that in Our Place. Some were physically unable to enter church buildings; others were not understood or welcomed. Some families persevered, but others withdrew. At this point the New Wine leaders asked members of the team to share with the wider Church what they had learned and how leaders in particular could welcome all people into their congregations. A number of seminars were held at the summer gatherings and this was followed by annual training days with a developed training package. The training day was often held at All Saints' Woodford Wells, the church led by Paul and Becky Harcourt. A number of churches invited members of the Our Place team to come and help them to grow in their understanding of the truths that had been explored over the summer, seeking practical ideas for applying them to their specific communities. Our Place was becoming a place from which learning could be shared.

One individual, Beth,[2] started volunteering with Our Place at age 15 and, through the opportunity to learn and receive training at United, decided to set up similar provision at her local holiday club. Beth discussed with the holiday club leadership team the Our Place model of inclusion and of enabling everyone to participate in mainstream activities, and was given the go-ahead to set this up. The holiday club had over 1,000 children and hundreds of volunteers, and soon an additional needs team was formed that enabled several children who were not from church backgrounds to access the holiday club and hear about Jesus. Through this holiday club, Beth started to build up relationships with local families who had children with additional needs. After a couple of years one of these families started coming to Beth's local church. Through this the local church began to increase its additional needs provision, and as this happened, more families with additional needs started to come. The church community was now modelling a way of welcome that saw beyond additional needs and viewed everyone as precious and valued in God's kingdom.

Like other teams at New Wine, the Our Place team was made up entirely of volunteers. Some came with knowledge and others had no experience of the world of additional needs at all. As people 'did life together', many lives were changed. Many of the team went on to train professionally and to work with those who have additional needs. Some changed their careers, and others went back to their churches to use what they had learned to welcome and include people there. Others set up charities for those with additional needs and their families in the UK, wrote books, or travelled abroad. Some became foster parents and yet others adopted children who had additional needs. Many received healing and learned to love and accept others; marriages were blessed, new skills were learned, and confidence was gained. Friendships were formed, courageous births and baptisms celebrated, and deaths were mourned. Heather comments:

Regardless of whether the change was a large one or not, no one who was ever part of Our Place came away without being changed in some way. Although we celebrate the things God has done in and through Our Place, we long for a day when Our Place will no longer need to exist because we will all have been changed.

ADULT PROVISION

Across the years, the additional needs support teams grew from being a small team supporting a small number of individuals, to supporting many families across the site at the summer gathering. By 2016, Our Place was supporting over 190 individuals with the help of 90 team members for each week of the United summer gathering.

As Our Place continued to grow, there was an increasing need for adult provision. Several of the individuals who had been children in 2003, when Our Place started, were now adults who continued to need support to participate and could no longer be a part of youth venues. In 2016 the team trialled a new adult provision called 'Access' with the aim being that adults could access the mainstream venues and participate in an accessible seminar stream which provided Bible teaching, ministry and worship in such a way that an adult with learning, physical, or mental health needs could more easily take part.

The team quickly found that starting this off led to a lot of interest and encouragement from families whose adult members had often struggled to participate at United. Naomi Graham explains:

Two families who bring their adult daughters to United were overjoyed with the possibility of their children being able to participate in something without needing their parents there to support them. Each year they had found with increasing frustration that there was not anywhere that their daughters could access the teaching and ministry at a level they understood which was not portrayed in a child-like way. Following the success of the pilot, we decided that we would officially launch Access in 2017.[3]

FOCUS

The Access team very much reflected the Our Place team and the heart for all individuals to have the opportunity to access United. The focus was on inclusion within mainstream adult

Access, started in 2016, provides an accessible seminar stream for adults with learning, physical or mental health needs

venues (Hungry, Impact, and the Arena) and in addition an accessible seminar stream run within the Access venue for the second half of the morning session. The heart of the Access team is to see adults being enabled to participate in all that is going on across the venues. There is an inclusion team that has a visible space within each adult venue and across the week at United, and its members support adults in a variety of ways to help them participate. From enabling individuals who use wheelchairs to have a space set up for them, to assisting individuals with hearing impairments so they find the best position to sit, through to helping individuals with learning needs to understand the talk by drawing it out to simplify it while it's going on – the team is very multifaceted!

Feeling at home is important to the team. Naomi explains:

> We have found that the Access seminar stream has also been an amazing opportunity for adults with a wide range of needs to feel at home in our venue. Within the seminars we have adults with physical disabilities sitting on our sofa to do their stretches, adults with significant learning disabilities filled with joy participating in worship, adults with Asperger's taking the time to be in a less busy and intense setting, adults with mental health needs taking comfort in being able to sit by a team member.

As part of setting up the Access venue, and together with the national increased understanding of additional needs and new policies relating to accessibility, it seemed appropriate to redefine New Wine's understanding of additional needs. The team saw additional needs as wide ranging; it could be a physical need, a learning need, a mental health need or an undiagnosed need – anything that had an impact on someone's ability to participate.

This seemed to really reflect God's heart for all people, no matter what their needs were. Again, Naomi comments:

> We see in Jesus' life that he is constantly bringing individuals back into community and enabling them to find home. Whether individuals have an official diagnosis or not, we want to be constantly enabling everyone at New Wine to be brought back into community and have that sense of home. This means that our remit goes beyond what may be seen as a typical disability and we have expanded our support to include needs such as mental health needs and extra support for adopted and fostered individuals. It feels like a reflection of God's kingdom that individuals with such a variety of needs can be supported across site at United. The Access venue is a small reflection of this, where we see adults with such a variety of needs come and worship and seek God as one community.

The Access venue has been set up next to Impact and the Arena at the summer gathering, and this has meant that adults can easily move between Access and the adult venues. A live link between Access and Impact has meant that in the evenings adults can participate in the main Impact session but from a quieter space.

HEALING MIRACLE

The members of the team have grown and increased in their experience and ideas for enabling adults to participate, and 2018 saw the first inclusion of a team within the Late Night Live (after-hours) venue in the Arena. This team was really significant in enabling adults to build relationships with one another, feel less lonely on site, and have the opportunity to share what God had being doing during the week. One such individual was Gemma.

She had some medical needs and a learning disability. At the start of the Late Night Live session she was chatting to one of the team members about her hearing – she was deaf and had only ever been able to communicate with her daughter through sign language. The team member prayed for her, and God restored her so that she could hear again. Her daughter was also at New Wine and there was a beautiful moment where Gemma was able to hear her daughter's voice for the first time.

Gemma's story is one of dramatic healing, but a large part of seeing God move within the accessible church team is in the stories that on the surface seem less dramatic, but for the families and individuals involved are just as significant. Naomi explains:

> We have seen adults feel safe enough to be without their parents for the first time in a long time. We have seen adults who normally spend every moment asking where their parents are, or asking to leave, who have been filled with the Holy Spirit and have a new joy and freedom in the way they worship which leads to others worshipping more freely. We have seen adults who find it hard to look at or connect with others have a moment of connection and a smile. Adults who have a physical disability feel valued because there is a space they can come and be. Church members have themselves been changed – people who have seen what we are doing and realized something more of how God can move when we choose to create a church that is more accessible.

SERVING ON SITE

One of the biggest impacts the Access team has had on the wider vision of United is through the part of the team that supports individuals with additional needs in serving on teams across the site. This was set up officially with the launch of Access in 2017 and saw around 15 individuals supported to participate in teams at United. The numbers increased in 2018 to around 30 individuals with additional needs serving on teams. The Access team provide the expertise and support needed so that team leaders can more easily enable individuals with additional needs to serve on their team. Heather was excited by this initiative:

> It was a joy to see young people and adults using their gifts to give to and serve others. It wasn't always easy, but everyone worked hard to make it possible. I know that I myself have grown in so many ways by serving on teams and giving to others. To prevent others from giving and serving keeps them in a place of being cared for, a place of weakness; it deprives them of the joy of serving and can prevent them from growing into the people God has made them to be.

Team members provide one-to-one support when necessary, and in addition there is a core team member whose role within the week is to check in with every individual with additional needs serving on a team. Naomi says:

> We see adults with learning disabilities, mental health needs, and physical needs being able to participate in teams across site. As we often see within our society, individuals with any kind of additional need are often perceived as less helpful or valuable within a team. Through providing support for individuals to participate at New Wine, we've been able to stand against this culture. We've found that many of the individuals we have supported have brought an incredible gifting and change to the team that they have served in.

One of these individuals is Tom. Tom has Down's syndrome, and before Access started at New Wine he spent most of his time in the food court or in cafés because he found it difficult to understand the other activities and participate in any of the adult venues. Now that Access has started, he finds that he is able to more easily feel a part of what is going on. He knows that if he doesn't understand something there will be a team member there who can explain. But Tom wanted to go further. In 2017 he started serving in the Tearfund café and he had an amazing time. Not only did Tom enjoy it but the team within Tearfund found that he also brought an incredible joy that enabled people to feel welcome when they came into the venue. The other team members loved having Tom on board and were really happy when he signed up to volunteer again in 2018.

Through running the accessible church ministries at United, the team have encountered individuals such as Tom. Lucy is another. In the world's eyes she could not walk, talk, eat or move, and yet she carries the most tangible sense of God's presence and peace with her wherever she is. Lucy has a close relationship with God that has moved many individuals who have met her.

APPOINTMENT

As the accessible church ministry started to grow, the national leadership of New Wine decided to appoint Naomi Graham as Head of Accessible Church Ministry in early 2017. The introduction of this role meant that more time could be given towards enabling the vision of accessibility to further develop within local churches. In this role Naomi provides training for local churches, answers questions, and helps to problem-solve where families, children's pastors, youth pastors and church leaders need support in terms of accessibility. Each year the team runs a national Accessible Church Conference which provides the opportunity for individuals across the country to share their experience, connect with one another, and leave with fresh training and vision from God as to what their ministry can look like.

Throughout the year God continues to do amazing things where, inspired by the Spirit, individuals are bringing kingdom changes to their local communities. One such story is Growing Hope,[4] a charity which Naomi herself has established, providing free therapy for children and young people with additional needs in partnership with local churches across the UK. Naomi was inspired, partly from her experience within New Wine, to continue her work as an occupational therapist but also to work increasingly with her local church. The charity offers hope for children to reach their developmental potential through free therapy services such as occupational therapy, physiotherapy, and speech and language therapy. It offers hope for families to grow relationally stronger and deeper through parenting courses and siblings' groups (such as the one run each year at United). The charity offers hope in Jesus through having therapists who work on a Sunday in order that church can be more accessible. Other charities and enterprises have been set up as part of the story of accessible church within New Wine, and there is an excitement to see all that God continues to do in the years ahead.

THE VALUE OF EVERYONE

The core of the accessible church team is the value that God sees in every serving individual, no matter what his or her needs or experience may be. This means that on team there will be individuals who have a lot of professional experience and others who have little or no experience. The vision is for the whole Church – for all believers to start to realize that they can make small steps that enable their church community to be accessible to everyone in their locality, no matter what the needs. For this reason, Naomi Graham wrote a book, *Love Surpassing Knowledge*.[5] This is a practical resource, based on her occupational therapy training and experience of running the accessible church teams, which celebrates all God has done through the New Wine family. The book enables church communities and church leaders to understand more about how different individuals connect with God, in order that in church meetings everyone can participate.

BREATHE

With the start of Access in 2017, the need for a place for parents and carers of adults with additional needs to meet together was also identified. The Our Place parents' venue had always focused on children and this led to a slight shift in 2018. A new separate venue within the accessible church ministry at United was set up, called Breathe. The name 'Breathe' was chosen because the vision of the venue was to see parents and carers of both children and adults with additional needs having the space to breathe – to take time to be themselves without having to be known as 'Jonny's mum' or 'Susie's dad', but also to take time to connect with one another. This facility has been a valuable resource for families, and many parents and carers come through the doors and participate in the seminar stream. In 2018 there were over 70 parents coming along each week. Naomi explains:

> Through many tears, and with much laughter, joy and even anger, we have seen change; encounters with Jesus, experiences shared, and marriages prayed for. We have had

discussions with church leaders and have given practical support. Several parents talk about how invaluable this space is where they feel they can honestly come as themselves, knowing that those they love and care for are well supported within Our Place and Access. We are excited to see all that happens as Breathe continues to grow and develop in the years to come.

The summer gathering of 2018 saw over 500 individuals and their families supported with additional needs throughout the two weeks of United by an amazing team of around 180 people. There is a clear intention to continue to celebrate and to develop all that God is doing in the lives of these precious individuals and families. Everyone gets an unconditional welcome.

12 Reflections on the journey

Paul Harcourt, National Leader of New Wine England, looks at the New Wine journey so far.

GIVING THANKS

On the last night of the last week of United 2018, as we prepared to say farewell to Shepton Mallet for the last time, we celebrated God's goodness and thanked him for the many ways that he had met us over 30 years. That morning we had made available simple cards, on which people could write their stories of how God had worked in their lives through the New Wine summer conferences. In the evening, hundreds of cards were brought forward during the worship, and they make incredibly moving reading:

- 'In 2006, we went forward for prayer about a physical ailment. As we received prayer for that situation, the ministry team member felt that she should ask for permission to pray for my wife's womb. We explained that we had been trying for a third child for five years, without success and with some distress . . . nothing happened, baby-wise, until the very last month in which we could conceive in time for the baby to be born before New Wine 2007. We were shocked but delighted when the scan revealed twins. Caroline went full term, and the twins were born in July 2007, just in time to make an appearance "on stage" in an evening celebration.'

- 'In March 2000 our son committed suicide, which devastated our whole family. I had been coming to New Wine for a few years already but decided in 2001 to serve on the Boulder Gang team. During the Workers' Celebration, I received amazing healing and a new sense of call to reach out to other troubled teenagers in my village. Just a couple of months later, I accepted a post as a part-time youth worker. Seventeen years later, the healing continues, and I still work with children, families and teenagers.'

- 'The first year I came, I had a powerful encounter with the Holy Spirit as a six-year-old. I kept coming, eventually graduating on to team so that I could give back what had been given to me. It was at New Wine that I heard God call me into youth work, and later to be a GP. Then four years ago, I signed up to speed dating and met my new husband. We now co-lead a church in Stoke. Our 11-month-old son is now in the children's groups and I am excited to see what God will do now in his life!'

- 'At our first New Wine in 1996, our eight-year-old son came back to the tent and found his dad had a bad headache. "Don't worry," he said, "I'll drainpipe him and God will heal him." He prayed as he'd been taught that week, one hand on his father and one hand raised to heaven, acting as a drainpipe for the Spirit, and the headache went! That was the beginning of his journey in faith. He is now a worship pastor.'

- 'Those Bible studies were so challenging and I decided to give everything to God. It was the beginning of a journey to leave our teaching jobs and go to Tanzania . . . we are not normally adventurous – it is something we could never have done apart from God.'

- 'At New Wine '90 I got a call to ordination in the Church of England. I am now a bishop – thanks! (I think . . .)'

Reading through the pile of cards, it's clear that the New Wine summer conferences have been a powerful place of encounter for so many. People wrote of finding faith, receiving healing, experiencing God's love and power in new ways, clarifying their own sense of call, or being inspired to start charities or church ministries. In numerous ways, the impact of those gatherings is still being felt. It has always been our heart that what happens when we gather would ripple out across the nation afterwards, and it has – indeed, across many nations, it would seem. I was especially struck by how many people had encountered God and gained a vision for what he might want to do back in their local community. Far from the allegation that is sometimes made, that Christian gatherings are essentially consumerist and indulgent, it seems that the New Wine story has been one of overflow and shared blessing. After 30 years, we are now also seeing the benefit of a generation of people who have grown up knowing nothing else, for whom kingdom values and a confident faith in the future of the Church come more naturally than they perhaps did for a previous generation.

LEADERSHIP INCUBATION

New Wine conferences have also been a tool that the Lord has used to grow leadership. I know that, in my own life, I've been able to grow significantly through some of the opportunities and responsibilities that come with an event on this scale. As a church leader, I have seen it proven many times that one of the most effective ways of training lay people and developing them in their own ministries is to encourage them to serve on one of the teams at the summer event. The large gathering serves as a hothouse for accelerated growth, and people always seem to come back enthused and inspired.

It is worth noting as well that many of the prominent Christian leaders in our country have deep roots in the New Wine family. As has been mentioned, Justin Welby, Archbishop of Canterbury, came with his family as a delegate for 12 years and, since becoming Archbishop, has returned to address the summer gatherings on three occasions. J John, Mike Pilavachi, Matt Redman, Tim Hughes and others have gone on to develop international ministries. John and Debby Wright now lead the Vineyard churches in the UK and Ireland. Other people who, like the Wrights, led Venue 2 include Frog and Amy Orr-Ewing, now of Latimer Minster, the Oxford Centre for Christian Apologetics, and Ravi Zacharias International Ministries. For many years, New Wine Youth was led by Gavin and Anne Calver, now known primarily for their leadership in the Evangelical Alliance and in Spring Harvest. The focus of people's ministries has sometimes developed, but the sense of remaining part of the wider New Wine family remains.

THE HEART OF NEW WINE

When Mark Bailey stepped down as National Leader in January 2016, we entered a six-month period of reflection on the journey that God had taken us on over the years. This included asking the fundamental question as to whether our season had ended, and

David and Mary Pytches, Melanie Patterson, John and Anne Coles and Paul and Becky Harcourt in the Main Arena, 2016

whether it was time to make way for new moves of God. (In the summer of 2018 the organizers of Soul Survivor announced that they would end their conferences in 2019 for just that reason.) Over the six months, though, there was a clear sense that God still had plans and purposes for New Wine in this nation. This was the sense not only of those inside the family, but also, and often even more strongly, of friends in other streams outside New Wine. By the time I was publicly announced as the new National Leader, I had the great blessing of inheriting a group of people to work with who had all – leaders, staff and trustees – recommitted themselves to New Wine as their family, and to the DNA that means there is a unique contribution that we make in the overall picture of what God is doing. As I now articulate this, I think that the DNA of New Wine is fourfold.

First, we hold a **kingdom theology of word and Spirit**. Our primary theological grid is that the gospel is the announcement of the coming of the kingdom of God. This was Jesus' message, which he both proclaimed in his teaching and demonstrated in signs and wonders. The gospel of the kingdom forces us to consider the whole of God's work of redemption and restoration, not simply our own individual spiritual lives or the growth of the Church. He is concerned with the whole of life, every aspect of his creation and of human society within it. Furthermore, Jesus made it clear that, although the kingdom is already at hand, we are to pray for the coming of the kingdom. As John Wimber taught in the early days: 'The kingdom is both *now* and *not yet.*' Theologically, this would be called an 'inaugurated eschatology' (the things that God intends for the future are already here in part) rather than the 'realized eschatology' common in more Pentecostal circles (where there is a greater emphasis on being able to receive it all now). No doubt this more nuanced theological position has helped New Wine bring renewal into many mainstream churches, in the UK and abroad.

Second, we place particular emphasis on **the ministry of the Holy Spirit**. It is the Spirit who brings the kingdom.[1] Our gatherings are characterized by passionate worship in God's presence with an expectation that we will encounter him and that he might, potentially at any moment, guide and direct the meeting in a different direction. Our teaching always leads to a time of response when people are invited to receive prayer or to respond in worship. Teaching and preaching, in our view, are opportunities not only to understand what is in God's word but also to hear him speak personally and directly to us. Preaching in that sense is a prophetic encounter between God and his people, but word and Spirit must be held together. The ministry of the Spirit is to enable us to gain revelation, but also to receive what God offers, and to empower us to be the people God declares us to be. He exalts Jesus, and he enables us to become more like him. So often, not least in my own life, I've seen how the course of someone's life has been changed through one of those encounters. We must never cease to invite his presence to become more powerfully felt in our gatherings.

For that reason, one of the characteristic responses in our celebrations has always been times of 'waiting on God'. For me, these times do several things. They give people time to transition from listening to teaching to responding personally, which often requires a different type of attention. They express our utter dependence on God – we are laying down our agenda and acknowledging that we want whatever he wants to do. Perhaps most significantly, they are a recognition that what truly changes lives is when he moves in power; so waiting is a statement of faith – like Jacob, we 'will not let go unless you bless us'.[2] In recent years, we have been rediscovering the power of these times.

Third, it has always been about **the local church**. The strapline 'Local churches changing nations', which was adopted in 2010, expresses this heart perfectly. David Pytches returned to the UK from Chile with a passion to see the revivals that he had seen in South America begin in his native country. For him, the renewal was always for the sake of mission, and it was rooted in the experience of the renewal of his own local church. My own history with New Wine might be instructive. I was attending renewal meetings for leaders at St Andrew's Chorleywood from the early 1990s, but, because we always went to visit my in-laws in the USA during the summer, Becky and I didn't make it to a

New Wine summer conference until 1996. That meant, for me, New Wine was a leaders' network before it was a gathering or event – just as it was for those who had been involved through most of the 1980s.

Even today, there is no formal way for a church to become 'part of New Wine': members of the church can come to our summer gatherings, and the church's leaders can sign up to the Network. With the conferences being so large, and such a great percentage of our financial turnover, there has often been a tendency for the summer conference to loom large in everyone's minds, but the heart of New Wine has always been for the renewal of the local church. The nation will not be changed by conferences; it will be changed by local churches. As a result, we have tried to have our conferences model what would be possible in the churches that were represented, just as the Pytches did in the beginning. We try to make things transferable, as much as possible. In the end, it's not about the two weeks when we gather; it's about the other 50 weeks when we engage our local communities with the good news about Jesus.

Some of the prophetic words that were given during the leadership transition of 2016 underlined this. One important word was that we should 'eat the fruit of our own tree'. This has been a reminder that we should be confident in celebrating what God is doing among us, rather than always thinking we need headline speakers from elsewhere. For a network like ours, the summer gatherings are as much about reinforcing the vision that unites us and celebrating what God has done in the year before as they are about receiving new input. I have had to explain to several journalists that 'United' isn't the theme of this year's conference – it's now the name of our annual gatherings every year! Again, some weeks after taking on the role of National Leader, I felt God say to me very clearly that we should 'bring our true spiritual children home', which I interpreted as an encouragement to bring over some of the wonderful leaders from other New Wine countries and learn from them.

That brings me, fourth and finally, to **the value of being family**. New Wine has always been a relational network. In many nations, the fact that no one needs to leave his or her denomination in order to join New Wine means that there is a great ecumenical aspect to this renewal which is very attractive.

As a family, centred on these few values, there is room for all sorts of variety, but a clear sense of being about the same things. Ministry is often a lonely or challenging place, but I know that many leaders find their local networks to be a great source of support and encouragement.

GENEROSITY

One mark of being family that has become increasingly apparent is generosity. John Wimber's original advice to David Pytches was that the kingdom works in this way: if you want more, give it away.[3] That has been seen in terms of relationships and in ministry, but also in financial giving. For much of our history, New Wine has been incredibly blessed to be able to take up offerings to give away to charities or to invest in further development, rather than simply to cover the running costs of the conference. Generosity on the scale that we regularly see is humbling and is, I think, a sign that delegates are aware both of having received much from God, and of feeling part of something bigger. There are things that we can do together as a family that we would never be able to do alone.

One of my favourite moments of all the New Wine summer conferences was in 2013. Our Ugandan speaker for one of the morning celebrations was unable to get a visa, so with two days to go we found ourselves needing a new plan. Mark Melluish told us about something he'd seen in the Thirst youth venue and asked a few of us what we thought about inviting that speaker, Steve Morris, a young youth worker from Chafford Hundred Community Church. It sounded as though God was doing something inspirational through his message about becoming a church that would be attractive to young people because it was a church that served the poor. At a day's notice, Steve found himself speaking in front of 6,000 adults in the Arena, our largest venue.[4] He spoke passionately about being 'all in', told everyone about his church's partnership with the Sozo Foundation in the poorest area of Cape Town, South Africa, and described the challenge of raising £40,000 for the Education Centre that they wanted to build.

Towards the end of the talk, with just a few minutes remaining, he told how he and his wife Diana had been challenged by God to give everything in their bank account into this cause, including what they had started to save as a deposit for a house. There was no plan for an offering, and at no point did he actually ask anyone to give, but as he spoke a woman walked to the front from the back of the Arena and placed £20 on the platform. As Steve spoke on, others began to do the same, until it turned into a flood of people, giving generously. Hastily placed buckets were overflowing with cash by the time he finished speaking. In those few minutes, around £30,400 had been given.

The next day, as word spread, this climbed to £34,000. The youth, who had already given £5,000 in their own meetings, itself

Steve Morris offering, 2013

a record, took up the cause and continued raising money through the week. One enterprising young man saw that the seminar programme included a seminar on generosity, and managed to raise £600 just from standing outside with a sign as people left the seminar! By the end of the week, over £50,000 had been given in total. Meanwhile, in Cape Town, on the day before Steve had spoken, American visitors to the Sozo offices had prophesied that 'God is going to provide every single penny for your new Education Centre'.

In that same year at United, hundreds of people came to faith, and many other wonderful things happened. There was a lady who came who had been blind for 18 months and had been given a guide dog. When she was prayed for, her sight was restored as it had been before. She was unable to recognize anyone she had met in the past 18 months because she was now seeing them for the first time and, in the midst of her rejoicing, her main concern was whether she would be allowed to keep her much-loved guide dog! This is our God, who is concerned about salvation and healing, about justice and the poor, about community and transformation. His goodness overflows from his people to the wider world.

I can think of several further stories from recent years – a couple who had been burgled just before their wedding, then had a honeymoon provided by a spontaneous offering when their story was told at United 2016; a youth worker who received exactly the make and model of car that he had been considering buying but was unable to afford, until someone said over the microphone that he had a car to donate because he'd received a new company car; or United 2017's significant offerings to accelerate the church planting that New Wine churches were engaged in.

These things encourage me that the DNA on which New Wine was originally based remains present and is continuing to bear kingdom fruit. The encounters with God through his Spirit ripple out into changed lives and transformed communities. Long may it continue.

13 New Wine tomorrow

Paul Harcourt, National Leader of New Wine England, considers what's next.

With such a great story to tell, a book like this could easily come across as a history of what God did in the past. I hope it is instead an encouragement that what God has begun continues to spread in influence and impact. There is an energy and a passion in the New Wine Network; new leaders are emerging from within, and new churches and streams of churches are joining the family. However, in the ever-changing landscape in which the Church witnesses to Jesus there are, of course, fresh challenges and opportunities.

UNDEFENDED LEADERSHIP

Part of the reason that New Wine remained healthy as it grew was, in many people's opinion, the balance between David Pytches' ministry and that of his wife, Mary. While David emphasized the outward drive of mission and evangelism, he was complemented perfectly by all that Mary was discovering about inner healing. In a 2011 interview, Mary explained that even though the Church was experiencing more of the Spirit, she was also discovering that people still had problems – even in the middle-class area where she now lived:

> People would turn up on my doorstep for a cup of coffee and a good cry and I'd pray for them. But I began to think, I need to know how to help them more than I'm doing. This isn't enough. So I started to do some counselling courses . . . and we started what we called first of all, Prayer Counselling but then we called it Pastoral Prayer Ministry.[1]

This turned into a significant contribution to the renewal, with Mary writing many well-regarded books on inner and emotional healing.[2] Working alongside my own wife, Becky, with her testimony and strengths in this area, I've come to realize that the emphasis on the outer journey of mission needs to be supported by the inner journey of personal renewal. This needs to be a dynamic that we never neglect.

New Wine has always been about encounters with Jesus through the Holy Spirit. As such, I believe that there has been, and always will be, an inseparable connection between the relationship with God and relationship with one another. Overall, I have seen (and received myself) incredible love and support between leaders, but it is a culture that needs to be guarded. In 2015 the Christian blogger Ian Paul was moved to write:

> I know most of the leaders in New Wine reasonably well, and we have warm and open relationships. They are responsive to feedback and listen to concerns – more than I think is realised. But for many who are further away in terms of relationship there is sometimes a sense that decisions have been made behind closed doors, and the reasons are either unclear or unconvincing. This is important for New Wine

itself – but it is even more important for the impact on local churches. I have known several New Wine churches which have been seriously damaged by arbitrary and authoritarian leadership – where people (usually men!) have mistaken strong leadership for unquestionable leadership.[3]

By their nature and gifting, many apostolic leaders are achievement oriented, which can easily tip over into a competitive spirit. The culture that we work hard to maintain today is one where competition is challenged, and cooperation is made the norm. We want to see the kingdom increasing as much as we ever did, but we're not concerned about who gets the credit. Jesus deserves all the glory. If we continue to make space for God and maintain love for one another, he will continue to move in power.

DIVERSIFYING

No one would look at New Wine and see a perfect reflection of the breadth of the Christian Church! In one sense, that it is entirely understandable. Movements always begin somewhere and then, travelling along relational lines, often spread most easily and quickly to areas where there is a similar culture. Having begun as the overflow of renewal in an Anglican suburban church, largely white and middle class, the New Wine family has for years been over-represented by similar churches. If God's call on New Wine is to play a bigger part in renewing the whole Church in this nation, then that has to be addressed.

We felt called in 2016 to rebalance the leadership of New Wine so that we were a better reflection of who we had become. For me, that meant, initially at least, broadening our leadership in terms of age, gender and geography. Being myself (at the time) in my late forties, and from a largely white, middle-class, London suburban church, I didn't exactly contribute to greater diversity in our leadership!

It's important to us as a network of leaders and churches that we are led by practitioners, but the balance between demanding local and national roles is always hard to strike. I proposed to the trustees that I would give slightly less time to the national role than my immediate predecessors but work with two part-time Assistant National Leaders, Mark Melluish and Kate Wharton. This immediately forced us to work as a team, enabled us to find roles for two exceptional leaders, and brought a broader perspective into our deliberations. We also tried to address the issue of age, gender and geography by increasing the size of the National Leadership Team and the range and location of churches represented. Mark Bailey had helpfully placed great emphasis on developing younger leaders, particularly through our INVEST ministry for those in their twenties, and we were pleased to build on that. Regarding women's ministry, despite a lead from John Coles to be known as being strongly supportive of women's ordination, New Wine historically has, like most conferences, been dominated by male voices. Project 3:28, founded by Natalie Collins in 2013 to report on the gender balance of UK Christian events, noted that in 2016 the percentage of women speakers in the 22 largest UK conferences and festivals was 36 per cent. At New Wine's summer conference this figure was 43 per cent and rose to 46 per cent in 2017. We continue to press forward on all of these issues, with a leadership that includes gifted men and women from a much greater range of contexts.

One area where New Wine continues to lag behind is in ethnic diversity. It would be almost unheard of now for us not to have black and Asian speakers on the platform at an event, but they often come as guests. While this initially reflected the churches from which the family gathered, it is probably the case now that there are more leaders from diverse ethnic backgrounds in New Wine churches than our leadership reflects. Possibly a factor has been that camping, as at Shepton Mallet, has historically been very much a white-British culture, but we are looking very intentionally at opening the way for a more diverse leadership. The move to the East of England Showground in Peterborough is partly so that we have a more centrally located gathering and can reconnect with northern churches that, after our conference at Newark closed, found Somerset too far. Hopefully, though, it will also provide an opportunity to connect more deeply with other cultures, bringing us within easy reach of thousands of hotel beds and making United more attractive to more people.

CLARIFYING AND LEANING IN

Nothing is as important as maintaining the DNA on which New Wine was founded, although from our encounters with God there will constantly be a flow of new things. The danger of anything that grows is that it slowly loses focus. With over 300 seminars in the programme each year, that could definitely be true of United. It is also true for the leadership network, which now includes about 3,700 leaders, but with an increasingly diverse definition of leadership, since 'kingdom ministry' is not only about building the Church. However, as much as we are called to bring kingdom transformation into every stream of culture, in our mind that is never to be divorced from the ministry of the local church.

Our strapline, 'Local churches changing nations', suggests our strategy – we aim to support the renewal of local churches so that they can have an impact on their communities and, ultimately, the nations with the good news. It's ideally in the local church where individuals' vocations into those areas of culture are nurtured and supported in community. In most cases, the fastest way to advance renewal in the Church is to work with the Church's leaders; so local church leadership remains a key focus for us, and we long to see Charismatic renewal going deeper and broader.

As we've asked ourselves how to increase the measurable progress towards our vision, I have found myself reflecting on how renewal can be sustained. God seems to intervene when times are darkest, but historically, these moves of God have often lasted for only a few years, and rarely beyond a generation. Without claiming that what God has done through New Wine is comparable, the contrast between the fruit of John Wesley's ministry and George Whitefield's seemed to speak to us. Both great revival preachers of the eighteenth century, as contemporaries their ministries were often compared. Most people would have concluded at the time that Whitefield's was the greater work of God. Despite this, towards the end of his life George Whitefield despaired that what he would leave behind would probably vanish: 'My brother Wesley acted wisely. The souls that were awakened under his ministry he joined in societies, and thus preserved the fruit of his labour. This I neglected, and my people are a rope of sand.'[4]

It seems that the wisdom needed is that of creating structures to support and sustain renewal, while never losing our focus on what actually produces life.

LASTING PRINCIPLE

Searching the Bible to see whether that was a lasting principle, I came back to the dark days immediately after the book of

Judges. In 1 and 2 Samuel, as God raises up Samuel and begins to establish his kingdom in Israel, it seems that this wider move of God was being spread and nurtured in companies or 'schools' of the prophets. Samuel clearly had a close relationship with them, and I suspect may have had a hand in founding them. Moving on a couple of generations, though, into the ministry of Elijah, these groups were being persecuted by King Ahab. Obadiah, a servant of Ahab but a devout believer, confides in Elijah that he has been hiding the Lord's prophets in caves to save their lives. Even though he knows this, Elijah still acts as if he is the only one whom God can use. His ministry, though heroic, is very much a one-man campaign. At his lowest moment, he even complains to God that he is the only one left![5] There seems to be a change in the ministry of his successor Elisha, and I wonder whether this is part of his greater impact.

Having a double anointing doesn't remove the need for being part of something bigger – just as the heart that John Wimber brought was not for a few extremely anointed super-stars but for the equipping of all the saints for kingdom ministry, where 'everybody gets to play'.[6] Throughout the chapters that describe Elisha's ministry, we hear frequently of 'companies of the prophets': in Bethel and Jericho,[7] at Gilgal[8] and at the Jordan.[9] It seems that renewal is sustained best when it is embedded. As a result, one passage that has helped the development of our thinking has been that last passage, 2 Kings 6. It is a simple story of a miracle of Elisha, making a lost axe-head float to the surface of the water, but it encapsulates some of these thoughts. In it, the prophets ask Elisha for his blessing on the establishing of a new school (which he gives), ask that he might come with them (which he does), and then experience the miracle where he returns a man's axe-head to him (symbolic of his ability to work effectively).

I've used this in a simple outline to articulate three priorities for us in the coming years: to establish centres of renewal to sustain and spread the move of God; to work on genuinely multigenerational leadership; and to not lose sight of individual personal renewal, our own and others'.

CENTRES OF RENEWAL

The most common challenge facing leaders in New Wine in past years was taking their churches through a process of spiritual renewal. Establishing openness to the gifts of the Spirit, developing prayer ministry, and having a new vision for intimate worship and encounter with God was the focus of much of our efforts. That remains the case in many places, but in the past decade there have also been incredible opportunities and encouragement for church planting. This has been a sea change in many denominations, whereby what was previously seen as imperialistic (and often resisted) is now actively encouraged.

Our aim must be to see a vibrant Spirit-filled church in every community, either by the renewal of already existing churches or the planting of new ones. Church planting takes an ever-increasing place in our thoughts, and in some ways is the natural result of renewal. As the Spirit comes, he restores life to his Church; as we come back to life and health, reproduction becomes a natural and normal part of life. Our 'Nation Changers' development fund is enabling us to make grants to church plants from within the New Wine family, as well as releasing people to come alongside leaders and work with denominational authorities. There is a lot of energy around to discover again what the apostolic gift might look like in today's Church, so that the Church can be extended and the gospel jump over barriers in today's society.

MULTIGENERATIONAL LEADERSHIP

Again, if the move of God is to continue passing from generation to generation, we realize that we need to give attention to the 'pipelines' of leadership. Being blessed with such inspiring and effective children's and youth ministry at United has clearly had an impact on the wider Church. Many young people graduate from being delegates to going on to team, and, as a result, gain both skills and vision for their lives. Some take this passion into the workplace and into the streams of culture (and are nurtured in our INVEST network); some give a year to invest in their discipleship (through the New Wine Discipleship Year, which 700 people aged 18 to 24 have undertaken); still others go forward into some form of Christian ministry (supported by our Leaders in Training network). We have workplace streams at United for those whose focus is there, and ministry streams to help develop lay ministry in local churches.

Where the 'pipeline' is most easily and effectively built is with those who will lead the local church – in many cases being a network that supports people at every stage of the journey, through training to first post to senior posts. We still have much to do, but several effective models of mentoring and learning communities are emerging and bearing fruit.

Multigenerational leadership means more than investing in each generation, though. It means allowing each generation to lead. Often in the past, leadership has been handed from one generation to another reluctantly, with those in the younger generation frustrated and waiting for their turn and an older generation feeling passed over and redundant now that the middle-aged are in charge! Instead, we are hoping to create platforms and programmes where all the generations can lead together, alongside one another, with each generation bringing its own strengths. Succession isn't about the stopping and starting of ministry but about changing the roles that we play in different seasons.

PERSONAL RENEWAL

I pray that God will protect us from ever writing a strategy that looks like an organizational plan. The story told in this book is not one of great leadership but of great faith in a great God (which is great leadership!). The strategy, so far as there has ever been one, has been this: we need God to come, and then we are determined to follow his lead to the best of our ability. Unless we are living that out ourselves in our daily lives, we are not going to be able to understand or enable that when we gather together. We know that we need the renewal of prayer, both personal and corporate, and have created a fourth adult celebration venue at the United conference from 2019 to reflect that.

We have also started to produce resources again as a network. New Wine's voice was heard in the early years through the books written by David and Mary Pytches, Barry Kissell, Bruce Collins, and others. In 2007 and 2008, Mark and Lindsay Melluish and Paul and Christine Perkin produced a syllabus for parenting children and teenagers. Then in 2010, John Coles wrote *Learning to Heal*[10] to express our prayer ministry model. More recently, we have begun to produce a greater number of resources again. Becky and I have written a couple of books on experiencing the Spirit-filled life,[11] John Peters has written on the ministry of the Spirit and on evangelism,[12] John McGinley has written on missional community,[13] and we have produced books on children's ministry and accessible church. This is a sign of a family that is confident that it has something to say, as well as an expression of our heart to see every individual and every church entering into the experience of renewal in the Spirit.

'GREATER THINGS'?

We are so grateful to God for our history, but we are also excited and expectant for our future. A new chapter begins with the summer gatherings moving for the first time to the East of England Showground. There is no great fear of losing the sense of meeting with God that we enjoyed at Shepton Mallet for 30 years, though. We have seen God do amazing things in many places, in local churches up and down this country, and in many other nations, some with cultures very different from our own. It's his work and, for as long as he has a role for New Wine in his purposes, we will seek to be faithful to the inheritance and steward what we've been given. John Wimber often said, 'I am loose change in his pocket; he can spend me any way that he wants.'[14] The name of 'New Wine' doesn't matter; it's all about his glory.

Could there even be 'greater things' in the years to come? It is hard to imagine. But then again, it must have been even harder for the disciples to imagine 'greater things' when Jesus first spoke those words in John 14: 'I tell you the truth, anyone who has faith in me will do what I have been doing. He will do even greater things than these, because I am going to the Father.'[15]

We have our part to play, but ultimately it's all about Jesus and what he does. It always has been. It always will be.

Notes

1 BEGINNINGS

1 Norman Grubb, *Rees Howells: Intercessor* (Cambridge: Lutterworth Press, 1952).

2 A MOMENT IN TIME

1 David Pytches, unpublished book contribution, October 2018.

2 <www.new-wine.org/profile> (accessed November 2018). See also Barry Kissell, *Springtime in the Church* (London: Hodder & Stoughton, 1976).

3 David Pytches, 'Fully Anglican, fully renewed', in *Riding the Third Wave: What comes after renewal?*, ed. Kevin Springer (Basingstoke: Marshall Pickering, 1987), p. 169.

4 David Pytches, in *Meeting John Wimber*, ed. John Gunstone (Crowborough: Monarch, 1996), p. 20.

5 David Pytches, in *Third Wave*, ed. Springer, p. 169.

6 Edward England, 'Do we need John Wimber?', *Renewal*, October/November 1985, p. 3.

7 Gunstone, ed., *Meeting John Wimber*, p. 8.

8 'Facing the canon', David Pytches interview with J John; produced by David Withers, Philo TV and UCB, 2014: <www.youtube.com/watch?v=4jW1Q88Sx88>.

9 6 and 7 June as recorded in Alex Twells, *Standing on His Promises:*

A history of St Andrew's Church, Chorleywood – a story of sustained renewal (Chorleywood: Twells Publishing, 1998), p. 222. Twells' book is ambiguous about the year, but all other sources and personal recollections date it to June 1981, such as David Pytches, *Living at the Edge: The autobiography of David Pytches* (Bath: Arcadia, 2002), pp. 268, 321.

10 Pytches, *Living at the Edge*, p. 254.

11 Mark Melluish, unpublished book contribution, November 2018, and throughout chapter.

12 Natalie Nash Diss, 'John Wimber: Assessing his theology, practice and legacy within the British Charismatic movement' (BA Hons Theology Dissertation, Durham University, 2017/18), p. 19.

13 Springer, ed., *Third Wave*, p. 169; Twells, *Standing*, p. 224.

14 Pytches, *Living at the Edge*, p. 264.

15 Ian and Meg Sinclair, 'ARM "Pytches" Spirit in Life Conference', *Anglicans for Renewal* magazine, Canada, summer 1996.

16 Twells, *Standing*, p. 224.

17 Twells, *Standing*, p. 224.

18 Gerald Coates, in *Meeting John Wimber*, ed. Gunstone, p. 80.

19 James Roberts, unpublished book contribution, October 2018.

20 Twells, *Standing*, p. 224.

21 Mary Pytches, interview with *Premier Christianity* magazine, 2011.

22 Twells, *Standing*, p. 223.

23 John Wimber, *Power Evangelism: Signs and wonders today* (London: Hodder & Stoughton, 1985), p. 148.

24 Mary Pytches, interview.

25 Carol Wimber, 'A wife's tribute', in *John Wimber: His influence and legacy*, edited by David Pytches (Guildford: Eagle, 1998), pp. 301-2.

26 J John, unpublished; book contribution, December 2018.

27 Pytches, *Living at the Edge*, p. 232.

3 RENEWAL

1 David Pytches, *Come Holy Spirit: Learning how to minister in power* (London: Hodder & Stoughton, 1985).

2 The conference was called 'The Church in the Power of the Spirit' and meetings were led by Michael Harper (Alex Twells, *Standing on His Promises: A history of St Andrew's Church, Chorleywood – a story of sustained renewal* (Chorleywood: Twells Publishing, 1998), p. 226).

3 Mark 2.22 (NIV, 1984).

4 GATHERING

1 Margaret Maynard-Madley, unpublished book contribution, October 2018, and throughout chapter.

2 Interview with Mike Pilavachi, October 2018, and throughout chapter.

3 Mark 2.22.

4 Alex Twells, *Standing on His Promises: A history of St Andrew's Church, Chorleywood – a story of sustained renewal* (Chorleywood: Twells Publishing, 1998), p. 268.

5 Twells, *Standing*, pp. 268-9.

6 Mary Pytches, interview with *Premier Christianity* magazine, 2011.

7 Barry and Mary Kissell, unpublished book contribution, October 2018, and throughout chapter.

8 J John, reflections on New Wine, unpublished, December 2018, and throughout chapter.

9 Interview by Tanya Raybould with Captain Alan Price, unpublished book contribution, December 2018, and throughout chapter.

10 Captain Alan Price with Liz Lunn, *Children in Renewal: Helping children follow Jesus, empowered by the Holy Spirit* (Stowmarket: Kevin Mayhew, 2000; originally Hodder & Stoughton, 1996).

11 Twells, *Standing*, p. 269.

12 Twells, *Standing*, p. 276.

13 *Independent* newspaper, 6 August 2009.

14 David Pytches, *Living at the Edge: The autobiography of David Pytches* (Bath: Arcadia, 2002), pp. 325-6.

15 Twells, *Standing*, p. 302. Improvements to the infrastructure at the showground meant, in time, single-week delegate numbers grew beyond this, and overall delegate numbers significantly increased beyond this with the addition of a second week.

5 DEVELOPING

1 John and Anne Coles, unpublished book contribution, October 2018, and throughout chapter.

2 Lindsay and Mark Melluish, *Family Time: The book of the course* (Eastbourne: Kingsway, 2002).

3 See Isaiah 40.3.

4 John Coles, *Learning to Heal: A practical guide for every Christian* (Milton Keynes: Authentic Media, 2010).

5 John and Anne Coles, *Making More of Marriage* (Chichester: New Wine, 2000).

6 GROWING

1 Christian A. Schwarz, *Natural Church Development: A guide to eight essential qualities of healthy churches* (Emmelsbüll, Germany: NCD Media, 1996).

2 Bob Jackson, *The Road to Growth: Towards a thriving Church* (London: Church House Publishing, 2005), p. 106.

3 John and Anne Coles, unpublished book contribution, October 2018, and throughout chapter.

4 Jackson, *Road to Growth*, p. 147.

7 SOUL SURVIVOR

1 Based on an interview with Mike Pilavachi, October 2018, and throughout chapter.

2 David Parker was a leader from Kansas City, brought over to Chorleywood to help with renewal. He and his family eventually returned to the USA to lead Lancaster Vineyard, California.

3 David Pytches, *Living at the Edge: The autobiography of David Pytches* (Bath: Arcadia, 2002), p. 330.

8 WORSHIP

1 Matt Redman interview, *700 Club*, 2009: <www.youtube.com/watch?v=YKoTN2IoGYY>.

2 David Pytches, *Living at the Edge: The autobiography of David Pytches* (Bath: Arcadia, 2002), p. 256.

3 Charles Whitehead, in *Meeting John Wimber*, ed. John Gunstone (Crowborough: Monarch, 1996), p. 41.

4 Terry Virgo, *No Well-Worn Paths: Restoring the Church to Christ's original intention* (Eastbourne: Kingsway, 2001), p. 152.

5 Les Moir, *Missing Jewel: The worship movement that impacted the nations* (Eastbourne: David C. Cook, 2017), p. 127.

6 Quoted by David Pytches, in *John Wimber: His influence and legacy*, edited by David Pytches (Guildford: Eagle, 1998), p. 69.

7 Matt Redman interview with writer Craig Borlase.

8 Matt Redman interview.

9 Interview with Mike Pilavachi, October 2018.

10 Mike Pilavachi, interview with Nicky Gumbel, *Focus*, 2014: <www.youtube.com/watch?v=kwzsWzwfqtc>.

11 Tim Hughes interview, *iBelieve Magazine*, October 2017.

12 Interview by Tanya Raybould with Tim Hughes, unpublished book contribution, December 2018, and throughout chapter.

13 Bryn Haworth, unpublished book contribution, October 2018.

14 Matt Redman, unpublished book contribution, October 2018, and throughout chapter.

15 Interview with Mike Pilavachi, October 2018.

16 <https://stories.new-wine.org/new-wine-worship-vision-

values–48dcf8b04b9e> (accessed December 2018), and throughout chapter.

17 Mary Pytches, interview with *Premier Christianity* magazine, 2011.

9 TO THE NATIONS

1 Bruce Collins, unpublished book contribution, October 2018, and throughout chapter.

2 @NWCymru on 2 November 2018 (tweet accessed December 2018).

3 1 Corinthians 12.7.

4 See Isaiah 40.3.

5 Acts 13.2.

6 Ephesians 2.20.

7 'Facing the canon', David Pytches interview with J John; produced by David Withers, Philo TV and UCB, 2014: <www.youtube.com/watch?v=4jW1Q88Sx88>.

10 CHURCH PLANTING

1 Roland Allen, *Missionary Methods: St. Paul's or ours – a study of the Church in the four provinces* (London: R. Scott, 1912; Grand Rapids: Eerdmans, 1962).

2 Roland Allen, *The Spontaneous Expansion of the Church and the Causes that Hinder It* (London: World Dominion Press, 1927; Cambridge: Lutterworth Press, 2006), p. 7.

3 C. Peter Wagner, *Church Planting for a Greater Harvest: A comprehensive guide* (Ventura: Regal, 1990), p. 11.

4 Bob Hopkins, *Church Planting: Models for mission in the Church of England* (Cambridge: Grove, 1988).

5 See Mike Starkey, *Ministry Rediscovered* (Abingdon: BRF, 2011), p. 26: <www.brfonline.org.uk/pdfs/9781841016160.pdf>.

6 John Coles, unpublished book contribution, October 2018, and throughout chapter.

7 Paper available at Regent University Library: <www.regent.edu/lib/

special-collections/wimber-files/JohnWimberCollectionBox21-26.
htm> (accessed December 2018).

8 David Pytches, *Living at the Edge: The autobiography of David Pytches*
(Bath: Arcadia, 2002), pp. 359-60.

9 Charlie Cleverly, *Church Planting: Our Future Hope* (London: Scripture
Union, 1991).

10 David Pytches and Brian Skinner, *New Wineskins: Defining new structures for worship and growth beyond existing parish boundaries* (Guildford:
Eagle, 1991).

11 Various, *Breaking New Ground: Church planting in the Church of
England* (London: Church House Publishing, 1994).

12 Various, *Mission-Shaped Church: Church planting and fresh expressions of
church in a changing context* (London: Church House Publishing, 2004).

13 <www.kxc.org.uk/story-vision> (accessed December 2018).

14 <www.churchofengland.org/about/renewal-reform/estates>
(accessed December 2018).

15 <https://joineden.org> (accessed January 2019).

16 <www.centreforchurchplanting.org> (accessed January 2019).

17 *Journal of Missional Practice*, Spring 2014.

18 *Journal of Missional Practice*, Spring 2014.

19 *Journal of Missional Practice*, Winter 2017.

20 <www.cinnamon.org.uk> (accessed January 2019).

21 <www.glochurch.org/out-history> (accessed December 2018).

22 <http://thebridgechurchplanting.co.uk> (accessed December 2018).

23 Various, *Mission-Shaped Ministry Course* (Cardiff: Fresh Expressions,
2013).

24 <www.poolemc.org.uk/reconnect> (accessed December 2018).

25 <https://acpi.org.uk/2017/09/20/farnborough/#more-598>
(accessed December 2018).

26 John McGinley, *Mission-Shaped Grace* (East Malling: River Publishing/
New Wine, 2017).

27 See 1 Corinthians 3.6.

11 OUR PLACE AND ACCESSIBLE CHURCH

1 Heather Holgate, unpublished book contribution, October 2018, and throughout chapter.
2 Other than the authors, names have been changed throughout this chapter.
3 Naomi Graham, unpublished book contribution, November 2018, and throughout chapter.
4 <https://growinghope.org.uk> (accessed November 2018).
5 Dr Naomi Graham, *Love Surpassing Knowledge* (East Malling: River Publishing/New Wine, 2018).

12 REFLECTIONS ON THE JOURNEY

1 Matthew 12.28.
2 See Genesis 32.26.
3 'Facing the canon', David Pytches, interview with J John; produced by David Withers, Philo TV and UCB, 1,900: <www.youtube.com/watch?v=4jW1Q88Sx-26>.
4 Steve Morris at New Wine: <www.youtube.com/watch?v=wIESEV3lW4Q&feature=youtu.be>.

13 NEW WINE TOMORROW

1 Mary Pytches, interview with *Premier Christianity* magazine, 2011.
2 These include *A Child No More* (London: Hodder & Stoughton, 1991); *Dying to Change* (London: Hodder & Stoughton, 1996); *Set My People Free* (London: Hodder & Stoughton, 1997); *Who Am I? Discovering your identity in Christ* (London: Hodder & Stoughton, 1999); *Rising above the Storms of Life* (Guildford: Eagle, 2002) and *Cry Freedom! Powerful restoration through the touch of the Holy Spirit* (Chichester: New Wine, 2008).
3 <www.psephizo.com> (accessed November 2018).
4 Ian Maddock, *Men of One Book: A comparison of two Methodist*

preachers, John Wesley and George Whitefield (Cambridge: Lutterworth Press, 2012), p. 83.

5 1 Kings 19.10, 14. The Lord has to remind him that he has reserved a remnant of 7,000 (v. 18).

6 Carol Wimber, 'A wife's tribute', in *John Wimber: His influence and legacy*, ed. David Pytches (Guildford: Eagle, 1998), pp. 301–2.

7 2 Kings 2.

8 2 Kings 4.

9 2 Kings 6.

10 John Coles, *Learning to Heal: A practical guide for every Christian* (Milton Keynes: Authentic Media, 2010).

11 Paul Harcourt, *Growing in Circles: Learning the rhythms of discipleship* (East Malling: River Publishing/New Wine, 2016); Paul and Becky Harcourt, *Walking on Water: Overcoming the obstacles to the supernatural life* (East Malling: River Publishing/New Wine, 2017).

12 John Peters, *Third Person: The work of the Holy Spirit* (East Malling: River Publishing/New Wine, 2017).

13 John McGinley, *Mission-Shaped Grace: Missional practices for missional disciples* (East Malling: River Publishing/New Wine, 2017).

14 <https://anitamathias.com> (accessed November 2018).

15 John 14.12 (NIV, 1984).

Index